DISHONEST MONEY

MONEY

Financing the road to ruin

BY JOSEPH PLUMMER

ISBN:1-4392-1411-5
ISBN13: 9781439214114

Visit DishonestMoney.com to order additional copies.

INTRODUCTION

The premise of this book is simple: Very smart and powerful people have created a *system* of financial control. With it, they are robbing you of your wealth, freedom and future. The average citizen, never taught how the system works, cannot effectively fight it.

If the premise of this book is simple, then its purpose is even simpler: Help the average citizen learn "the system" so they can protect their wealth, freedom, and future. ...Stop the thieves before they steal *everything*.

To achieve this purpose, we'll cover the following in common language:

The Federal Reserve System, the International Monetary Fund, the World Bank; who created them and who benefits? Inflation, deflation, booms, busts, BAILOUTS, depressions and recessions; what are they, what causes them and who benefits? Honest money vs. dishonest money; how are they different and who benefits? The CFR, the Trilateral Commission, the European Union, a North American Union, One-World government...who benefits?

By the end of this short book, the reader will be familiar with these terms, will know "who benefits" and (more importantly) will know *who pays*...

CONTENTS

ACKNOWLEDGEMENTS

"A writer who steals the work of another is called a plagiarist. One who takes from the works of *many* is called a researcher. That is a roundabout way of saying I am deeply indebted to the efforts of so many who have previously grappled this topic. ...Without the cumulative product of their efforts, it would have taken a lifetime to pull together the material you are about to read."

– G. Edward Griffin [1]

It's only fitting that this book begins with the quote above. It is taken from "*The Creature from Jekyll Island*" by G. Edward Griffin. Although I've read many books, papers, and articles; listened to lectures and viewed documentaries on the topics we're about to discuss, I have found no single resource better than Mr. Griffin's book. As such, I have written "Dishonest Money" to serve as a *beginners guide*. (What you're about to read only scratches the surface.) For a much more thorough account, please purchase and read *The Creature from Jekyll Island*. To buy directly from the author, please visit: www. RealityZone.com/creature.html

---

1   Unless otherwise noted, all *indented* quotes (like the one at the top of this page) are the words of G. Edward Griffin.

CHAPTER 1
Money is Power

• "Permit me to issue and control the money of a nation, and I care not who makes its laws." **-Mayer Amschel Rothschild**

• "We shall have world government...The question is only whether world government will be achieved by consent or by conquest." **-James Paul Warburg**

• "Some...believe we are part of a secret cabal working against the best interests of the United States, characterizing my family and me as 'internationalists' and of conspiring with others around the world to build a more integrated global political and economic structure — one world, if you will. If that is the charge, I stand guilty, and I am proud of it." **-David Rockefeller**

• "The powers of financial capitalism had a far-reaching aim, nothing less than to **create a world system of financial control** in private hands **able to dominate the political system of each country** and the economy of the world as a whole. This system was to be controlled in a feudalist fashion by the central banks of the world acting in concert, by secret agreements arrived at in frequent meetings and conferences. ...**Each central bank...sought to dominate its government** by its ability to control Treasury loans, to manipulate foreign exchanges, to influence the level of economic activity in the country, and to influence cooperative politicians by subsequent economic rewards in the business world." **-Carroll Quigley** (Emphasis added.)

If you were alive in 1910, you wouldn't have been invited to the meeting. Don't feel bad. Only a handful of the world's 1.7 billion inhabitants at the time were important enough (and powerful enough) to be summoned. You also wouldn't have known anything about what was discussed. In fact, you would have never known that a meeting took place. Despite the enormous impact on your country's future, the scheme to create a new "monetary system" was none of your business. (As such, the powerful men who organized the meeting went to great lengths to keep it a secret.)

What you *would have* known in 1910 is the names of the *powerful men who organized the meeting*. They were: Rockefeller, Rothschild, Morgan and Warburg. Through their banks and investment firms, these four names represented 25% of the world's wealth. ...And in those days, the *common people* kept a close eye on these "super-rich bankers." Citizens in the United States and Europe knew the game. They knew how the financial elite used their power to dominate industries and *influence* government. If word had gotten out that these extremely powerful competitors were meeting secretly, people would have feared they were combining forces to gain even *more* power and control. (The people would have been right.)

So, this is where the story of the Federal Reserve System begins. The banking empires of Rockefeller, Rothschild, Morgan and Warburg arranged a top secret meeting and sent representatives on their behalf to the privately owned *Jekyll Island*. To prevent the men from being recognized, Jekyll Island's permanent staff had been sent on vacation and carefully screened temps took their place. Each participant was sworn to secrecy and instructed to *only* use their first name to further conceal their identity. (Nearly two decades passed before any of them publicly admitted they'd participated in the meeting.) In that meeting, the financial elite created, for themselves, the monetary system that we live under today.

Those involved:

1. The head of J.P. Morgan's Bankers Trust Company
   - Benjamin Strong
2. Senior partner of the J.P. Morgan Company
   - Henry P. Davison
3. United States Senator, Chairman of the National Monetary Commission, business associate of J.P. Morgan and father-in-law to John D. Rockefeller Jr.
   - Nelson W. Aldrich
4. Assistant Secretary of the U.S. Treasury
   - Abraham Piatt Andrew

5. Representing William Rockefeller and the international investment banking house of Kuhn, Loeb and Company and president of the National City Bank of New York (The most powerful bank at the time)
   - Frank A. Vanderlip
6. Representing the Rothschild banking dynasty in England and France, partner in Kuhn, Loeb and Company, brother of Max Warburg who was head of the Warburg banking consortium in Germany and the Netherlands
   - Paul M. Warburg

Powerful competitors "joining forces" to achieve a common goal is nothing new. What *is* new about this particular meeting is the sheer magnitude of its success. By first writing the laws that would govern their industry (and then using government to pass and enforce those laws) the men of Jekyll Island created a system of generating profit and control that is unrivaled in all of human history.

By setting their differences aside, they could now direct their combined power against anything that stood in their way. Common enemies like emerging competition, currency drains and bank runs were targeted first. These *enemies* had limited the expansion of their wealth and power. Now they could be dealt with.

Emerging Competition

From the years 1900 to 1910, the number of banks operating in the United States had more than doubled to over twenty thousand. Most of the new banks had sprung up in the South and West and this was costing the large New York banks an increasing percentage of their business. However, in a "free market economy" there was little the New York bankers could do (legally) to stop this. So, as is often the case with unimaginably rich and powerful people, they co-opted the power of government. By rewriting the "rules and regulations" in their favor, they could systematically weaken and eliminate their competitors.

Another form of "competition" came from self-financing. That is to say, businesses were using their own profits to finance new projects instead of using bank-borrowed funds. (From 1900 to 1910, seventy percent of funding for corporate growth came from within.) As such, the banks were being cut out of the equation and businesses were becoming increasingly independent. Even the federal government had gotten into the act. Worse than "not borrowing," the government was actually paying off the national debt. Less and less debt equals less and less profit for the banks...this was a trend that had to stop.

To gain control of this problem, the bankers needed a system that allowed them to bypass the free market and manipulate interest rates directly. For instance, to encourage debt over saving and self-financing, they could tip the interest rates down. (Low interest rates encourage people to borrow and spend recklessly – more borrowing equals more debt, more debt equals more profit for the banks.) Then there is the option of being able to *raise* interest rates at will. This kind of control was a powerful tool they couldn't do without.

Bank Runs

One of the greatest threats a bank faces is known as a "bank run." It should be noted that if banks actually ran a legitimate business, "bank runs" wouldn't be a problem. But they don't run a legitimate business and so bank runs *are* a problem. To understand what a bank run is, it helps to understand the fraudulent nature of our banking system. In essence, it is this:

When you deposit money in a bank, you expect the bank to keep your money safe until you want to withdraw it. If 100 people deposit 100 dollars in a bank ($10,000 total) the expectation is; the bank now has $10,000 in their vault. Under these circumstances, there would be no problem if all 100 people showed up on the same day to withdraw their $100. The bank could simply take the $10,000 out of the vault, return $100 to 100 people and that would be the end of that.

The problem is the bank never has anywhere near as much money on hand as it *owes* to its depositors. Instead of keeping your money in their vault, the bank *loans it out* to others. As if that isn't bad enough, they then (based on the rules of our current system) are allowed to loan out even more money they don't physically have. (Don't worry; we'll cover this ridiculous fact of modern banking in Chapters 6 and 8.) When all is said and done, it isn't uncommon for a bank to have only a couple dollars on hand for every $100 (or more) that it *owes* to others.

If the public keeps its money in the bank, as it usually does, no problems arise. But if something spooks the public, or if more than a few percent of the population simply decides they'd like to have their money, the scam is exposed. When word gets out that the bank is stalling or unable to pay its depositors, the problem intensifies. Suddenly masses of people converge on the bank in an attempt to "get their money" (this is known as a bank run.) The bank of course doesn't have anywhere near enough money to return to its depositors and bankruptcy usually follows. Sadly it's the depositors who end up "paying the price."

A normal human would look at the system and say it needed to be corrected. Banks shouldn't be allowed to loan out depositor's money without the depositor's consent. Nor should the bank be permitted to create even *greater* financial obligations by *loaning out* even more money it doesn't actually have. But who said any of this was going to make sense? We can't forget the banking business is a *business*. Its current structure wasn't created for the benefit of the "normal humans" who don't understand it. There is a lot of profit to be made in loaning out money you didn't have to earn, so figuring out a way to protect the inherently fraudulent system (rather than correcting it) was one of the main goals of the Jekyll Island conspirators.

Currency Drains (Important note on usage[2])

A currency drain is very similar to a bank run. The bank owes more money to other people than it has on hand and, as

---

2 Regarding the term *Currency drain*: Today, the term "**currency drain**" is almost always used to describe the removal of currency from the banking system and the loss of "excess reserves" that this causes. However, here the term is used to describe a problem that banks faced "**Pre**-Federal Reserve System." (Prior to the creation of the Federal Reserve System, it was not uncommon for reckless banks to "inflate deposits" far more than others. This invariably led to a "drain" on the reckless bank's currency, as described here.)

a result, it is driven into bankruptcy. With a currency drain however, instead of *depositors* lining up at the bank's teller window seeking their money, now it is other *banks* lining up seeking what they're owed.

As an easy example, imagine for a moment there are only two banks: Joe's Bank and Mary's Bank.

Let's say that I (Joe) have a $100 balance in my checking account. I decide I want to purchase Mary's computer and she agrees to sell it to me for $100. Rather than go to my bank to withdraw cash, I simply write Mary a check.

When Mary cashes my check at *her* bank, the $100 she is given comes out of *her bank's* available cash. In other words, Mary's bank is temporarily "out" $100. The transaction isn't complete until Mary's bank sends the check I wrote to *my bank* and demands the $100 from my account.

Now imagine my bank agrees to "loan me" $1,000 it does not have. (Again, we'll cover how banks literally "create money out of nothing" in chapters 6 and 8.) For now, suffice to say my bank simply types "1000" into their computer and, by doing so, adds $1,000 to my checking account balance.

With my new $1,000 balance I go to Mary and ask if she'd like to sell her old lawn tractor. She agrees. I write her a check for $1,000, she deposits it in her bank, and her bank returns the check to my bank for payment. However, this time my bank cannot come up with the cash it needs to pay Mary's bank. This is the basic idea of how a "currency drain" manifests. Currency drains come about when banks make more promises to "pay money on demand" than they can keep.

Of course, in the real world, there are many banks and many customers. While I'm writing a check for $1,000 that will be deposited in Mary's bank, somebody from Mary's bank might write a check for $1,000 that will be deposited in mine. In this case, the two checks would cancel each other out (each bank owes the other $1,000.) Because no money would need to be transferred to balance these transactions, there wouldn't be any "drain" on either bank's available currency.

Another scenario where a bank would not have to worry about experiencing a currency drain would be: I write a check from my bank to somebody who also banks at my bank (or one of its many other branches.) When the person I wrote the check to deposits it at one of the "Joe's bank" branches, the bank only needs to subtract some digits from my account balance and add some to the depositor's account.

But back to the main point: Rigging the system to protect against currency drains (rather than correct the underlying fraud that causes them) was one of the *"great achievements"* of those who brought us our "Federal Reserve System."

Banker's Heaven

As the system stood in 1910, some banks were more reckless than others about "loaning money" they didn't have. (Remember, banks make money on loans…the more loans they can issue and collect interest on, the more profit they earn. There is always a great temptation to *loan* as much as possible.) The predictable result of reckless banking was this: Customers would *borrow* from a reckless bank and then write checks on their newly created account balance. Those checks would wind up deposited with *other banks* and those *other banks* would demand payment. Inevitably, the reckless bank would be drained of all its available currency (all of its customers' cash deposits) and would go belly up.

To illustrate this a little further, imagine we have a cautious bank and a reckless bank. The cautious bank has $10,000 of its own money on hand for every $10,000 in "checking account" money it creates as loans. As a result of keeping cash reserves equal to 100% of its loans, it will never have a problem with too many checks coming in from other banks. It will always be able to meet its obligation to produce cash because its obligations are 100% backed by its cash reserves.

Our other bank (the reckless one) has $10,000 in cash on hand, but it isn't happy with earning interest on only $10,000 in loans…it wants to earn interest on $500,000. So it starts issuing "loans" (creating new checking account balances "out of thin air" for its loan customers.) As those customers start writing checks, and those checks start finding their way into other banks, the inevitable "currency drain" begins. The bank goes broke, depositors lose everything, and the *free money* (interest/profit earned on money that existed only as keystrokes in a computer) is over for the bankers involved.

Historian John Klein explains: "The financial panics of 1873, 1884, 1893, and 1907 were in large part…triggered by the currency drains that took place in periods of relative prosperity when banks were loaned up."

In other words, banks were walking closer and closer to the edge of how much money they could loan out (without sufficient cash to back those loans) and this practice led to repeated panics and the failure of some 1,748 banks over a couple decades. Again, rather than do the obvious (fix the fraudulent system), our banker friends were intent on expanding their profits and protecting themselves from the naturally occurring losses.

The Bankers' immediate "wish list" probably looked something like this:

1. Stop the growing influence of smaller "rival banks." By pushing them out, they could expand their control over the nation's financial resources.
2. Make the money supply "more elastic." (Make it easier for them to create large amounts of "money," out of thin air, to loan.)
3. Create a system that allowed them to manipulate interest rates. (With this power, they could entice borrowers and reverse the trend of people using their own profits to finance growth.)
4. To help stave off currency drains and bank runs, encourage banks to maintain the same *loan* to reserve ratio (If everyone only *loans out* TEN TIMES their cash reserves, the system would be easier to manage than if some banks were "recklessly" loaning out fifty or one hundred times their reserves.)

5. Consolidate the inadequate cash reserves of the nation's individual banks into one large reserve. (That way, if a member bank was experiencing a "run," cash from the consolidated reserve could be sent over to satisfy withdrawal requests.)
6. If the entire system should come crashing down, have a mechanism in place to shift the losses from the bankers to the taxpayers.
7. Convince the people (and Congress) the "new system" would protect and benefit the public.

To achieve these goals, the bankers needed a strong alliance backed with legislation and sustained by the power of government. A near perfect model was already up and running in Europe; it was simply a matter of exporting it to the United States.

Still, that would prove easier said than done. Unlike today, voters knew better than to allow a handful of banking interests to centralize power, interfere with competition and manipulate the free-enterprise system. They had no faith in what was commonly referred to as "the money trust" and these men *were* "the money trust." So, selling the scheme became an issue of wrapping everything in the right words and then pouring on the propaganda.

How they sold it to the public

Anger over recent panics and bank failures (caused by the fraudulent banking system already in place) was used to stir up demands for "monetary reform." After creating sufficient public outcry, the Jekyll Island conspirators stood ready with the "solution" they had drafted.

The cartel[3] would operate as a central bank, but for the purpose of public relations the word "bank" would not be used. To gain the public's trust, "the system" was given the appearance of a federal agency. (In reality, the system is owned and controlled by private interests.)

The plan's initial structure was kept somewhat conservative, but it contained plenty of wiggle room to get it *just right* over time. To avoid the appearance of a "Wall Street centralized power structure" it was designed with regional branches scattered about the country. To create the appearance of academic approval, university professors were employed to tout its merits.

Last but not least, the VERY MEN who conspired to make the plan a reality attacked and condemned it publicly. This final step convinced the public it was "bad for the money trust" and hence "good for them." From start to finish, the banker's PsyOP worked like a charm.[4]

What began as a secret plan in 1910 became a reality on December 23, 1913. "The Creature from Jekyll Island"

---

3 A "cartel" is basically an alliance between businessmen who seek to monopolize a certain market or industry. (It's especially dangerous in this case since the "monopoly" involves our nation's money supply.)
4 A psychological operation (or PsyOp) is defined as: *"Techniques used... to influence a target audience's emotions, motives, objective reasoning, and behavior... in order to... reinforce attitudes and behaviors favorable to the originator's objectives."* You'll be hard pressed to find a better definition of the weapon used against the American people to secure adoption of The Federal Reserve System.

(The Federal Reserve System) was signed into existence and it has been feeding on us all ever since.

Although "The Fed" was supposedly implemented to stabilize our economy and benefit the public, a look at its history shows it has done anything but.

> "Since its inception, it has presided over the crashes of 1921 and 1929; the Great Depression of 1929 – 1939; recessions in 1953, 1957, 1969, 1975, and 1981; a stock market "Black Monday" in 1987; and a 1000% inflation which has destroyed 90% of the dollar's purchasing power." -TCFJI[5]

That latter point (a 1000% inflation which has destroyed 90% of the dollar's purchasing power) is an outdated figure. As of this writing, it is actually closer to **97%!** It's impossible to assess the full impact of the Federal Reserve System without taking inflation into account.

Inflation has been called a "hidden tax" because it reduces your purchasing power just as surely as government taking part of what you've earned (in taxes) reduces your purchasing power.

If you earn $10,000 dollars and the government takes $3,000 of it, your purchasing power has been reduced by 30 percent. If you earn $10,000 and a government-sanctioned inflationary policy reduces the purchasing power of your money by 30%, the impact on your earnings is the same; you've suffered a

---

5 TCFJI stands for The Creature from Jekyll Island. As stated on the *acknowledgements* page, all "indented quotes," unless otherwise noted, are the words of G. Edward Griffin and are taken from his book, The Creature from Jekyll Island.

loss in purchasing power equal to $3,000. It's no different than if they had simply taken the $3,000 from you.

Unfortunately, very few people understand this and that works to the advantage of those who profit from the system. Think about it. You'd be mad if somebody stole $3,000 from you; you'd know exactly how much of your money was missing and you'd want to go after whoever took it. But when was the last time you complained about the erosion of your purchasing power? When was the last time you tried to figure out how much of your money has been stolen via inflation over the past 5 or 10 years? When was the last time you "went after" those responsible?

We will cover inflation in greater detail in upcoming chapters. For now, we'll keep it very simple: As the Federal Reserve facilitates the reckless expansion of our money supply (inflating the amount of currency and credit in our economy) the ever increasing volume of money decreases the value of our dollars. As the value of our dollars goes down, the number of dollars it takes to buy things goes up.

In short, the Federal Reserve System has failed miserably in its *stated* objectives. It has not *stabilized* the economy and it does not protect and benefit the public. Furthermore, based on the inherently fraudulent nature of the system, it can be reasonably argued that its stated objectives were never its REAL objectives at all.

> "When one realizes the circumstances under which it was created, when one contemplates the identities of those who authored it, and when one studies its actual performance over the years, it becomes obvious that

the System is merely a cartel with a government façade."

Antony Sutton, Professor of Economics at California State University sums it up this way:

> "Even today,....academic theoreticians cover their blackboards with meaningless equations, and the general public struggles in bewildered confusion with inflation and the coming credit collapse, while the quite simple explanation of the problem goes undiscussed and almost entirely uncomprehended. **The Federal Reserve System is a legal private monopoly of the money supply operated for the benefit of the few under the guise of protecting and promoting the public interest.**" (Emphasis added)

If "the system" cannot meet its stated objectives, and if those stated *objectives* were never more than bait (used to *get us on the hook,*) then there is no reason why this "Creature" should be permitted to breathe another day. Congress created it. Congress can, *and should*, kill it.

CHAPTER 2
Something for Nothing

So far we've established that The Federal Reserve System was created in secrecy by a handful of powerful men. We know they sought (and secured) the power of government to maximize their profits and shift the inevitable losses of their fraudulent banking practices onto the backs of the American people. Now, let's briefly walk through some of the mechanisms that enable them to do this.

The first step is to create money out of nothing. For now, we only need to know that the bankers can "loan out" money they do not possess. So for instance, let's say you need to borrow $200,000. The bankers simply type "200,000" into your checking account and *poof*, they just created $200,000.

As soon as this $200,000 is loaned to you, it is entered into the bank's books as an asset. (You signed a contract that says you owe the bank $200,000 and it is assumed you will pay it back.) However, the loan is also entered into the bank's books as a liability. (It is assumed you will go out and spend your recently created $200,000 worth of checkbook money and your bank will be *liable* for those checks.) In other words, many of the checks you write will wind up in other banks and that means the issuing bank (your bank) will owe, potentially, up to $200,000 as those *cashed* checks start rolling in.

Being able to earn interest on money created out of thin air is a sweet deal for the bank. If it takes you 30 years to repay your loan (as is the case with a typical mortgage), the bank will *earn* hundreds of thousands of dollars in interest on the money it *loaned* you. But $200,000 is small change. Let's look at the kind of money they'd much rather be dealing with. Let's consider a loan of say $200 million.

The bankers still create the money out of nothing, they still enter the loan as an asset and a liability, and they still earn profit from interest charges. There is hardly any difference between typing 200,000 into a database and typing 200,000,000 (only a few extra keystrokes). However, those "few extra keystrokes" amount to one thousand times the profit. To put it another way: If you were a banker, would you rather process 1,000 loans at $200,000 each or would you rather find just ONE customer that you could *loan* $200,000,000 to?

From a "paperwork to profit" standpoint, the $200 million loan is the clear choice. However, there is at least one good reason why a bank might prefer making 1,000 smaller loans to making just one big loan. That reason is: It's far less likely that all 1,000 loans will go bad – one giant loan of $200 million puts an awful lot of eggs in one basket. It creates a greater risk.

Some might jump in here and say: "But they created the money out of nothing! What difference does it make if the loan isn't paid back?" While it is true that the money was created out of nothing, loans that go into default can still cause serious problems for the bank. In short: When somebody defaults on a loan, that "asset" is wiped from their books but the "liability" side of the equation still exists. All that checkbook money is still out in circulation and the bank is obligated to redeem those checks. (Additionally, the lost "loan asset" puts the bank at risk regarding certain regulatory requirements.)

If the person who defaulted has nothing of value to seize, the bank must get the money to cover its obligations from somewhere else. If the bank's profits or stockholder equity aren't sufficient, the bank becomes insolvent and the gravy train (collecting interest payments on *money* the bankers created out of thin air) can come to an abrupt end.

Under normal circumstances, this would encourage banks to be very cautious about the loans they approve, especially big loans. Oh, but those BIG loans are so much easier and they generate so much profit! Assuming you had the power; why not devise a system that protects the bank from insolvency in the event the *really big* loans go bad? Why not indeed...

The Federal Reserve System, The Federal Deposit Insurance Corporation (FDIC) and The Federal Deposit Loan Corporation all exist to do just that. They stand by to "guarantee" the massive loans that banks make to governments and corporations. The argument for rescuing these loans when they go bad is the same argument that is always used: "It's in the public's best interest." (I guess we're supposed to ignore the fact it is *the public* that ends up paying for the bank's irresponsible lending, in effect subsidizing and encouraging more "irresponsible lending" in the future.)

To put that another way: If you're a banker and all of your really enormous loans are eligible for a *bailout*, but your smaller loans are not, doesn't this encourage you to *go big*? It's kind of like telling a gambler: *"As long as you bet really, really big, there is no need to worry; your losses will be insured."* Not only does the gambler stand to make more on larger bets (as the banker stands to make more on larger loans), but the inherent RISK is no longer an obstacle.

Do we encourage "responsible gambling" (or responsible lending) with this approach? And if the answer is no, is it fair to encourage irresponsible behavior knowing full well the financial consequences are going to be shifted to somebody else?

> "The end result of this policy is that the banks have little motive to be cautious and are protected against the effect of their own folly. The larger the loan, the better it is, because it will produce the greatest amount of profit with the least amount of effort. A single loan to a third-world country netting hundreds of millions of dollars in annual interest is just as easy to process – if not easier – than a loan for $50,000 to a local merchant...If the interest is paid, it's gravy time. If the loan defaults, the federal government will "protect the public" and...will make sure the banks continue to receive their interest."

The goal is Perpetual Debt

Before continuing, it's important to note that banks don't get to keep the money they "create out of nothing." If a bank creates $200,000 out of nothing today, loans it to you, and then you pay the loan back next week, the bank doesn't get to keep the $200,000 you paid them. Whatever they create for loans, they must also destroy when the loan is repaid. (Again, we'll cover this process in greater detail in Chapter 8.)

What the bank DOES get to keep is the interest it earns on the money it creates. So the process goes something like this: You ask to borrow $200,000 to purchase a home. The bank "creates" the money and then loans it to you at 8% interest over 30 years. By the time you make your final payment, the bank will have *earned* $328,000 in interest. $328,000 is a pretty nice profit when you consider the $200,000 *loan* you paid interest on was created by typing some digits into a computer.

To understand this is to understand the dirty little secret of banking. Bankers don't really want customers who *pay off* their debts; they want customers to remain heavily *in debt*. (The bigger the debt, the better.) Governments are especially attractive in this respect. Not only do governments never pay down what they owe (guaranteeing indefinite profit on the original loan amount), they also can't seem to stop spending money they don't have. That is to say, they never stop *adding* to the debt they've already accumulated. As the debt forever climbs, so too does the bank's profit.

Suddenly the game of loaning insane amounts of money to governments and corporations starts to make sense. Why should the bank care if the borrower is buried in debt? What difference does it make if the BIG borrower's revenue stream barely covers interest payments? Remember, those "really, really big loans" are protected. Once there is a system in place for shifting the loan obligations onto others, the only logical objective (from a profit standpoint) is to get the borrower "on the hook" for as much money as possible. When the inevitable happens (the borrower becomes unable or unwilling to make any more payments), it's time for the final play: Get the citizens to pick up the tab.

Consider this a simplified illustration of the process.

A "high-risk" loan of $250 million dollars is made to the government of a third-world country. The government spends the money and is soon unable to keep up with its multi-million dollar monthly payments. The bank (after "careful consideration") decides to *help* the government by providing yet another loan. Once again, the loan payments resume and all is well. However, before long the new loan is exhausted and now the country is in even worse trouble. If it couldn't make payments on the first loan, how can it make payments on the TWO loans it now has? Simple; the bank agrees to create even more money out of nothing and loans *that* to the country. This process can go on for decades. With each new loan the bank increases both its "asset" (the amount of money it is owed) AND the profit it earns on the ever-increasing interest payments.

Eventually, the borrower realizes that interest payments alone are eating up nearly all available revenue. There is no way the enormous debt will ever be repaid and bank offers for "helpful" new loans are rejected. What is the bank to do? If the loan goes into default, it stands to lose both the "loan asset" and the highly lucrative interest payments...

After intense negotiations, the bank *kindly* agrees to "reschedule" the loan. (That means reduce the interest rate and extend the loan period.) In reality, this is hardly a concession. Sure, by reducing the interest rate and extending the loan period the bank makes it easier for the borrower to pay, but it has only postponed the inevitable. Sooner or later, the day of reckoning will come. But for now, this move keeps their huge asset on the books and keeps the interest rolling in.

At long last the day of reckoning does arrive. The borrower realizes he can never repay what is owed and flatly refuses to continue paying millions of dollars a month in interest to the bank. The jig is up. Or is it? ...Time for the final play.

G. Edward Griffin explains:

> "The president of the lending bank and the finance officer of the defaulting corporation or government will join together and approach Congress. They will explain that the borrower has exhausted his ability to service the loan and, without assistance from the federal government, there will be dire consequences for the American people. Not only will there be unemployment and hardship at home, there will be massive disruptions in the world markets. And,

since we are now so dependent on those markets, our exports will drop, foreign capital will dry up, and we will suffer greatly. What is needed, they will say, is for Congress to allow him to continue to pay interest on the loan and to initiate new spending programs which will be so profitable he will soon be able to pay everyone back. The bank... will agree to write off a small part of the loan as a gesture of its willingness to share the burden. (This however represents) ...a small step backward to achieve a giant stride forward. ...this modest write down is dwarfed by the amount to be gained through the restoration of the income stream..." (On money created out of nothing.) *Text in parenthesis added.*

This final play, the "bailout," shifts the financial burden from its rightful owners (the borrower and the bank) onto the backs of the American people. Where there would have been consequences for recklessly loaning so much money, there are now billions of dollars to be made in interest payments on those *"reckless"* loans. Where the bank's *"mistakes"* would have surely cost them, those same *mistakes* become an enormous stream of guaranteed profit. Thanks to the bailout, the "loan asset" will not be lost, the revenue stream will continue without further interruption, and it's you and I who'll pay for it all.

"Through a complex system of federal agencies, international agencies, foreign aid, and direct subsidies"[6] money extracted from the American people goes first to the borrower, and

---

6   Griffin

then is sent to the banks to service the loans. Most of this money does not come from taxes, but rather is "created out of thin air" by the Federal Reserve System. As the newly created money flows into the banks and then out into our economy, it dilutes the purchasing power of our money. Confiscation of our purchasing power (via inflation) is the result.

Even with this elaborate system standing by to bail out the banks, there is still plenty of opportunity for the banks to *loan* themselves into insolvency. For instance, bank runs are always a real threat because the banks keep only a small fraction of their customer's deposits on hand. The bank not only loans out the money you've deposited with them, they also create more money (checkbook obligations to pay) out of thin air. If even a small percentage of the people get spooked and show up at the same time to withdraw their deposits…you know the rest. Sure, the Federal Reserve was created to help the bank in situations like this; but there are limits. If the bank has dug itself too big of a hole, it's time for the FDIC play.

FDIC to the rescue:

FDIC stands for Federal Deposit Insurance Corporation. The concept behind this agency seems noble enough: If a bank presses its luck too far and ends up going broke, its customer's deposits are insured up to $100,000 each. Given a choice, most people would rather do their banking at an FDIC insured bank. Better to get your money back if the bank goes broke than not.

Unfortunately, just as the banks never keep anywhere near the amount of money in their vaults that they owe their customers, the FDIC has nowhere near the amount of money it claims to *insure* on hand in the event of a banking collapse. How thin are the "reserves" standing by to rescue the people from irresponsible banking? Just about as thin as one could imagine. Not 50%, not 30%, not 15%, or even 5%...more like 1%.

As if that isn't bad enough, that paltry 1% doesn't even exist in the form of cash. By law, the bank fees paid into the "FDIC fund" must be invested in Treasury bonds. In other words, it is "loaned" to Congress which of course promptly spends every penny. (If the FDIC truly "insures" anything, it's a steady supply of money flowing into Treasury bonds for our politicians to spend.)

One major bank failure could easily wipe out the so-called FDIC fund in an instant. Not to worry though, the fund is "backed by the full faith and credit of the federal government." Well, doesn't that make you feel warm and fuzzy inside? The same federal government that doesn't have any money; the same government that is currently borrowing more than a billion dollars a day to try and support its spending programs...

So what happens when the FDIC has exhausted its ability to cover depositor's losses? The government (with *full faith* in its *credit*) must borrow it. So it sells more I.O.U.'s (Treasury securities) and whatever the public doesn't buy, the Federal Reserve agrees to purchase. But the Fed has no money either...no problem. Whatever amount of money the

Fed needs to buy the government securities will simply be "created out of thin air" and *presto*: the FDIC is now funded. The newly created money floods into the economy, the purchasing power of our currency goes down, and through the hidden tax of inflation we all pay the price. Isn't this fun?

CHAPTER 3
The Bailout

Enough with the *set up*, let's take a look at the Federal Reserve System in action. Limiting our focus to a period of roughly 20 years (1970 through 1990), we'll pick out some of the more interesting and well-documented bailouts.

While reading, keep in mind that there are "bigger and better" bailouts in the works right now. As long as it's profitable for the financial elite to make these kinds of *"mistakes,"* the stories that follow will never end.

Penn Central Railroad

In 1970, Penn Central was America's largest railroad. It employed 96,000 people, had a weekly payroll of $20 million, and was on the verge of bankruptcy. If ever there was a candidate for a "protect the public" bailout, this was it. One thing to keep in mind as we proceed, many of the large banks that had loaned Penn Central into inescapable debt also had bank officers on Penn Central's board of directors. In other words, Penn Central was *"mismanaged into insolvency"* by the very banks it owed money to. They helped dig the giant hole from which the company (and the bankers) would eventually be rescued.

The House Banking and Currency Committee Chairman, Wright Patman, conducted an investigation in 1972 and found:

> "The banks provided large loans for disastrous expansion and diversification projects. They loaned additional millions to the railroad so it could pay dividends to its stockholders. This **created the false appearance of prosperity and artificially inflated the market price of its stock** long enough to dump it on the unsuspecting public. Thus, the banker-managers were able to engineer a three-way bonanza for themselves. They:
>
> (1) received dividends on essentially worthless stock, (2) earned interest on the loans which provided the money to pay those dividends, and (3) were able to unload 1.8 million shares of stock – after the dividends, of course, – at unrealistically high prices." (Emphasis added.)

Even *if* the railroad had been permitted to go into bankruptcy, the bankers would have been protected. Penn Central's assets would have been sold off and, as in any liquidation, the banks would have been paid first. The stockholders, on the other hand, could only hope to get some scraps (if anything remained at all) after the company's debts had been cleared. (Knowing this, the individual bankers who engineered the crisis had already dumped most of *their* stock prior to public disclosure of the railroad's problems.)

But why go the bankruptcy route when the Federal Reserve System had been created for precisely this kind of situation?

En masse, they descended on Congress; Penn Central's executives, bankers, union representatives, even the Navy Department, all speaking of the dire threat to the "public interest" - even national security - should Penn Central be allowed to go under. Congress patriotically responded by ordering an immediate pay raise of 13 ½ percent for all union employees, adding yet another financial burden to the already failed company. And with the "Emergency Rail Services Act" they authorized $125 million in federal loan guarantees.

Of course neither of these moves solved the underlying cause of Penn's financial problems and the railroad was "nationalized" (*"...a euphemism for becoming a black hole into which tax dollars disappear"-Griffin*) in 1971. By 1973 it had been split into two divisions: Amtrak and Conrail. Amtrak handled passenger services and Conrail handled freight.

By 1998, Congress had dumped $21 Billion into Amtrak and its liabilities *still* exceeded its assets by roughly $14 billion. In 2002, it was burning up roughly $25,000 per hour (24 hours a day, 7 days a week) of taxpayer's money.

Fortunately, the government sold Conrail in 1987. Since returning to the private sector, it has managed to turn a profit. Now it pays taxes instead of just consuming them.

Lockheed

Also in 1970, the nation's largest defense contractor, Lockheed Corporation, found itself mired in nearly half a billion dollars of debt. To save the giant from bankruptcy, and of course save the banks from losing a huge asset and stream of income, a group of concerned interests descended on Congress. The banks, Lockheed management, stockholders and labor unions all explained how jobs would be lost, subcontractors would be put out of business and national security jeopardized if Lockheed was unable to borrow more money and fast. (…Money that no bank wanted to loan absent a government guarantee.)

The government responded with a bailout plan of $250 million in loan guarantees, increasing the company's debt by over 50%. But wouldn't this insane increase in debt put the company at even greater risk of insolvency? Under normal circumstances it would, but not in this case. Why? Because now the government (on the hook for $250 million) had all the incentive in the world to steer lucrative defense contracts to Lockheed so it could pay its bills. Again, rewarding failure and punishing success. Those contractors that operated their business more efficiently didn't have the added leverage of saying, "If we fail, then you (the government) have to come up with hundreds of millions of dollars." It would be foolish to think that didn't come into play when deciding who was awarded a contract and who wasn't.

Lockheed did eventually go on to pay back its loans, but in this case it really wouldn't have mattered if they didn't. As G. Edward Griffin explains:

> "…every bit of the money used to pay back the loans came from defense contracts which were awarded by the same government which was guaranteeing those loans. …Taxpayers were doomed to pay the bill either way."

First Pennsylvania Bank

When a bank has loaned itself so far into a hole it cannot escape, the FDIC has a few ways it can intervene:

1) The *payoff* option: Insured depositors are paid off and the bank is allowed to slide into bankruptcy and its assets are liquidated. If you're a small bank with no political clout, this is what you're likely to get.

2) The *sell off* option: The insured depositors are paid off and arrangements are made to have a larger bank assume control of the failed bank's assets and liabilities. The bank's name changes, but there is no interruption in service and few people notice what has occurred. Maybe you're a medium-sized bank, maybe you've got a little more clout; in either case, this is a better option if you can get it.

3) The *bailout* option: The bank does not close and ALL depositors (insured and not insured) are paid off. If you're fortunate enough to secure this option, odds are you're a very large and well-connected bank. The significance of *all* depositors being paid off is this: Large banks are apt to have many *uninsured* accounts. (That is, accounts exceeding $100,000 each and accounts held outside the US.) Since the FDIC only charges participating banks a percentage of *insured* deposits, the large bank ends up collecting on insurance it never had to pay for. That huge savings gives an even bigger competitive edge to the larger banks. But that should come as no surprise; it's exactly the way the Jekyll Island group wanted it.

As you might have guessed by now, First Pennsylvania Bank was a BIG bank. In 1980, with assets exceeding $9 billion, it ranked 23rd in the nation. After bungling itself into insolvency, its final move was predictable. (The bankers went to Washington with their bailout request.) As if warnings of catastrophic consequences in Philadelphia were not enough, they spun tales of an international financial crisis should First Penn not be saved. First Penn, they claimed, would act as the first falling domino in a string of collapses that would circle the entire globe.

Needless to say, nobody wanted to be responsible for refusing to do whatever they could to avert such a catastrophe. In response, the FDIC granted First Penn a one-year $325 million interest-free loan. That, by itself, saved the bank a couple million per month. After the interest-free year, the loan converted to about half the market rate (many millions more saved). Banks that were tied to First Penn loaned an additional $175 million and offered a 1 billion line of credit. (The FDIC insisted on this move. It wanted to show that the banking industry *had faith* in the bailout.) The Federal Reserve offered those banks low interest funds to make sure there was plenty of *faith* to go around. In the end, failure was again rewarded and everyone made lots of money (except the citizens who subsidized it all).

Continental Illinois

Sad to say, First Penn was literally *child's play* compared to Continental Illinois. With 12,000 employees, offices in countries all around the world, and $42 billion in assets, it ranked 7th in the nation. For a while, it seemed unstoppable.

(Continental Illinois') "...net income on loans had literally doubled in just five years and by 1981 had rocketed to an annual figure of $254 million. It had become the darling of the market analysts and even had been named by *Dun's Review* as one of the five best managed companies in the country. These opinion leaders failed to perceive that the spectacular performance was due, not to an expertise in banking or investment, but to the financing of shaky business enterprises and foreign governments which could not obtain loans anywhere else."

Continental Illinois had invested heavily in Argentina, Mexico, and a string of high risk businesses. In 1982, as the Argentine and Mexican debt crisis came to a head and a series of corporations went into bankruptcy, the bank was hit hard. But just as Penn Central Railroad had done 12 years earlier, the bank did all it could to project an image of "business as usual." It continued to pay dividends that it really couldn't afford and it made good use of what the bank's chairman called "The Continental Illinois Reassurance Brigade." (That would be the bank's employees, all around the world, doing what they could to calm the nerves of its depositors and stockholders.)

The move worked for a while, but by 1984 the bank's bad loans had reached $2.7 billion and that figure was growing. With literally hundreds of millions of dollars in lost revenue, paying stockholders and maintaining an image of prosperity was becoming increasingly difficult. It was just a matter of time. News of the bank's shaky financial situation began to trickle out (a rumor here, a rumor there) and before long, the floodgates were blown wide open.

The World's First Electronic Bank Run

To see Continental Illinois from the outside, you'd never know what was happening. You'd never know, as the sun rose on Wednesday May 9th 1984, that a bank run of historic proportions was underway. On that one day, 1 billion dollars in Asian money was withdrawn silently, electronically. By Friday, the bank was forced to borrow $3.6 billion from The Federal Reserve to cover escalating withdrawals and by the following Friday, total withdrawals exceeded $6 billion!

> "The Continental run was like some modernistic fantasy: there were no throngs of hysterical depositors, just cool nightmare flashes on computer screens..." –Ron Chernow

> "Inside the bank, all was calm, the teller lines moved as always, and bank officials recall no visible sign of trouble – except in the wire room. Here the employees knew what was happening as withdrawal order after order moved on the wire, bleeding Continental to death...." –Irvine Sprague

Now would be a good time to mention: If Continental would have been allowed to collapse, its stockholders would have been wiped out, its depositors would have lost a fortune, and the financial world would have been badly shaken. But who says that would have been a bad thing? The losses would have stirred anger and the anger would have driven demands for change. It would be near impossible to hide and excuse the inherently fraudulent nature of the system under such scrutiny and legitimate outrage. The long-term benefits to our nation (of undoing the flawed system) would have been enormous. But of course, no such thing was ever considered. "The System" had been created for a reason and this was it. It was time for the Fed and FDIC to work their magic which means it was time for the citizens to pay.

Earlier we mentioned large banks are most likely to be bailed out (have ALL their depositors paid off) *AND* are also most likely to benefit the most from a bailout as they're apt to carry many *uninsured* deposits. Continental proved to be a shining example. A full 96% of Continental's exposure was uninsured when *help* arrived. Or to put it another way, the bank had only paid to insure 4%, but now "to protect the public" it would be covered 100%.

> "The final bailout package was a whopper. Basically, the government took over Continental Illinois and assumed all of its losses. Specifically, the FDIC took $4.5 billion in bad loans and paid Continental $3.5 billion for them. The difference was then made up by the infusion of $1 billion in fresh capital in the form of stock purchase. The bank, therefore, now had the federal government as a stockholder controlling 80% of its shares, and its bad loans had been dumped onto the taxpayer. ...By 1984, "unlimited liquidity support" had translated into the staggering sum of $8 billion. By early 1986, the figure had climbed to $9.24 billion and was still rising. While explaining this fleecing of the taxpayer to the Senate Banking Committee, Fed Chairman Paul Volcker said:

'The operation is the most basic function of the Federal Reserve. It was why it was founded.'"

Behind the creation of all this money sat the Federal Reserve System. Interesting that the Fed is known as the "Lender of Last Resort" when, in reality, it has no money to lend. No money, that is, until it creates some out of thin air, pours it into our economy and, through the hidden tax of inflation, confiscates purchasing power right out of our pockets.

As G. Edward Griffin explains "...*the System was created at Jekyll Island to manufacture whatever amount of money might be necessary to cover the losses of the cartel.*" And that is exactly what it does – for the "big guys." If you're a *little guy*, don't expect any favors.

During the first 6 months of 1984, while Continental was getting the royal treatment, 43 smaller banks learned the following lesson first hand: As a small bank, the only deposits that are covered are the ones you paid to insure and you can rest assured you won't receive any bailout offers. If you're in trouble, you've got little choice but *sell out* to a larger bank. (Score another advantage for the Jekyll Island conspirators. Drive out or buy out the competition; either way, they win.)

The Housing Market

Up until now, we've seen how the penalties of mismanagement and fraud (in business and banking) can be turned into great rewards. Now we'll have a look at the Savings and Loan industry (S&L) and how government promises of "A house on every lot" led to S&L bailouts of epic proportions. Suffice to say: "You ain't seen nothin' yet."

During the Great Depression, Marxists blamed the capitalist system for the country's dire financial situation. Spouting visions of a socialist utopia, they were starting to gain popular support. Many of our nation's politicians, formerly champions of personal responsibility and individualism, quickly learned the advantages of preaching government paternalism.

Suddenly, it was more than "OK" to push for socialist policies in America, it was now politically profitable. There seemed to be something in it for everybody. The elites were more than happy to consider implementing a *planned economy*; after all it was they, the wealthy and well-connected intellectuals, who would be in charge of *the planning*. The politicians had everything to gain. Not only could they vastly expand the power and control of government (which in turn increased their own power and control) they could do so under the banner of "doing what was right for the country." Last but not least, a large percentage of the population (financially crushed and demoralized by what they were *told* was the "instability of the free market") was ready to accept just about anything. So many Americans were ruined by the Depression; it wasn't too hard to sell the idea of a little *government help*.

Franklin Delano Roosevelt (FDR) came to represent the epitome of the new American politician.

> "Earlier in his political career, he had been the paragon of free enterprise and individualism. He

spoke out against big government and for the free market, but in mid life he reset his sail to catch the shifting political wind. He went down in history as a pioneer of socialism in America. ...While the Marxists were promising a chicken in every pot, (Roosevelt's) new dealers were winning elections by pushing for a house on every lot."

Through the FHA (Federal Housing Authority), private home loans would now be subsidized by the federal government. At first, many people who might not have been able to afford a home *did* benefit from FHA assistance. However, it wasn't long before these new "FHA subsidized" buyers began to drive up the price of homes and that offset any real advantage.

As another step to help the housing market, banks were *required* to pay less interest to their depositors than S&Ls. This drove deposits into the S&Ls, increasing the amount of money available for home loans, but it also *decreased* the amount of loan capital available for all other industries. (Great if your business is part of the home industry; not so great for everyone else competing for the same investment dollars.)

It was also about this time the FDIC (mentioned earlier) and the FSLIC (Federal Savings and Loan Insurance Corporation) first came into being. If there were to be losses, the people no longer had to worry; "The government would pay for it." Too few realized, then as today, that the government doesn't pay for anything. Every dollar is confiscated in one way or another from what others have earned. Consider the irony of government forcing you to give it money (or taking it through inflation) so it can *protect you* from losing your money.

Unfortunately, government *solutions* are always wasteful and often counterproductive. Even if you accept the idea that government programs and policies are *intended* to serve us (rather than *intended* to secure and expand the power of the elite) you don't have to be a genius to calculate the dismal results.

The war on drugs, the war on terror, a house on every lot; whatever "solution" the government comes up with, it tends to create more problems than it solves. And with more problems come more proposed *solutions*, more demands for increased funding, more demands for greater control. In short: The more the government fails the more money and power it confiscates. If those who benefit from this backward system aren't "failing on purpose," they ought to be.

The consequences of government meddling in the housing market took a long time to manifest, but by the time they arrived, the results were disastrous. The costs of complying with government regulations alone have been estimated at 60% of ALL S&L profits. In addition:

> "...the healthy component of the industry must spend over a billion dollars each year for extra premiums into the so-called insurance fund to make up for the failures of the unhealthy component, a form of penalty for success. When some of the healthy institutions attempted to convert to banks to escape this penalty, the regulators said no. Their cash flow was needed to support the bailout fund."

As the Federal Reserve began raising interest rates, the S&Ls (to continue attracting depositors) had to offer more attractive rates themselves. By December of 1980 S&Ls were paying nearly 16% on their money-market certificates. This would be fine if they then loaned that money out at a higher percentage, but they weren't. In fact, the average rate they were earning on new mortgage loans was only 12.9%. Worse, many of their old mortgage loans were only producing 7% or 8% and still others were in default (paying nothing at all.) Simple math illustrates the S&Ls were already broke and only going deeper in the hole.

Under normal conditions, few people would want to put their money in a failing institution. But with S&L deposits *fully insured*, "normal conditions" didn't exist. The only thing that mattered to those making deposits was that hefty 16% *risk-free* return on their money. Brokerage firms with huge blocks of cash to invest were especially happy with the arrangement. Backed by the "full faith and credit" of the US government, there was nothing to lose and everything to gain by putting their money into the S&Ls.

By now, we all know what backs the "full faith and credit of the federal government." Consumer Reports, wise to the scheme, put it this way: *"Behind the troubled banks... stands "the full faith and credit" of the Government – in effect, a promise, sure to be honored by Congress, that all citizens will chip in through taxes or inflation to make all depositors whole."*

Using clever accounting techniques (read that as *fraudulent accounting techniques*), an all-out effort to make the S&Ls

look healthy and prosperous was put into play. This only postponed the inevitable and greatly increased the final carnage. Over a period of just 6 years (1980 – 1986), 664 insured S&Ls went belly up. The government, true to form, was in way over its head. It simply couldn't afford to close all the thrifts because it didn't have the funds to pay off their depositors. In March of 1986, the FSLIC had only 3 pennies for every dollar of insured deposits. Just prior to 1987, that dropped to **two-tenths of 1 penny** for every dollar.

> "Keeping the S&Ls in business was costing the FSLIC $6 million per day. By 1988...the thrift industry as a whole was losing 9.8 million per day, and the unprofitable ones—the corpses which were propped up by the FSLIC—were losing $35.6 million per day. And, still the game continued."

By 1989, the FSLIC no longer had two-tenths of a penny for every dollar, instead it now had nothing. It too was insolvent. The time had come for the government to spring into action (and boy did it.) With the passage of "The Financial Institutions Reform and Recovery Act" (FIRREA), $300 billion was allocated to "protect the public." $225 billion would come directly from taxes or inflation and $75 billion would be siphoned off the healthy savings and loans. It was by far the biggest bailout ever. And, of course, with the enormous failure came an excuse to add more controls (more government) to the whole inexcusable mess. We now would have the Resolution Trust Oversight Board, the Resolution Funding Corporation, The Office of Thrift Supervision, and the Oversight Board for the Home Loan

Banks. On signing the bill, President Bush (Sr.) proudly announced:

> "This legislation will safeguard and stabilize America's financial system and put in place permanent reforms so these problems will never happen again. Moreover, it says to tens of millions of savings-and-loan depositors, *'You will not be the victim of others' mistakes. We will see—guarantee—that your insured deposits are secure.'"*

Would you be surprised to discover the bailout estimate was a little low? Probably not since Congress ALWAYS gives low-ball estimates to get their bills passed. (Once a bill is signed into law, that's when the figures start to magically *adjust themselves* upward.) How much is a little low? $10 billion? $25 billion? $100 billion? No, more like $225 billion. Yep, by the time all was said and done the total bailout cost sat at just over half a trillion dollars. (Roughly $525 billion total.) It sure is good to know that we "will not be the victim of others' *mistakes*."

Cooking the books

The world of "government regulation" is really a sight to behold. What would be blatant criminal activity if you or I did it becomes an accepted (and encouraged) way of *doing business* when our government protectors are at the helm. Now is as good a time as any to provide some examples of how the government helped the S&Ls *cook the books*.

Cooking the books is all about making income or assets look bigger than they actually are. (It can also include making liabilities and losses look smaller than they actually are, but for now let's focus on the "assets" end.) Any fool knows it's great to have assets and the S&Ls needed all the assets they could get. So the government, in its infinite wisdom, decided it was OK for the S&Ls to put a dollar value on the amount of "community good will" they had. (That is not a joke.) Poof, just like that they created $2.5 Billion dollars worth of *assets* for themselves. **Add it to the books!**

Another asset problem the S&Ls had: They found themselves "upside down" on many of their loans. In other words, Pete borrowed $125,000 to purchase his home, but because of falling real estate prices, Pete's house was now only worth about $85,000. In the real world, the S&L only had an asset worth $85,000 backing the $125,000 loan. That little inconvenience was overcome by allowing them to ignore true market value and instead list value based on the original loan amount. **Add it to the books!**

We know the FSLIC had promised to bail out the ailing S&Ls should they get themselves into trouble. Surely there were some *assets* that could be squeezed out of that "full faith and credit" right? Absolutely! "Certificates of net worth" were issued based on the government's promise to pay and the S&Ls were allowed to then list the value of those certificates as assets. **Add it to the books!**

But *clever accounting tricks* (fraud) can only achieve so much.

> "The moment of truth arrives when the S&Ls have to liquidate some of their holdings, such as in the

sale of their mortgages or foreclosed homes...
That is when the inflated bookkeeping value is
converted into the true market value, and the
difference has to be entered into the ledger as a loss.
But not in the never-never land of socialism where
government is the great protector." Dennis Tucker
explains:

> 'The FSLIC permits the S&L which sold the
> mortgage to take the loss over a 40-year period.
> Most companies selling an asset at a loss must
> take the loss immediately: only S&Ls can
> engage in this patent fraud. Two failing S&Ls
> could conceivably sell their lowest-yielding
> mortgages to one another, and both would raise
> their net worth! This dishonest accounting in
> the banking system is approved by the highest
> regulatory authorities.' "

A lot of people have heard of the Savings and Loan crisis,
some might even understand who has ultimately had to "pay
the costs of others' mistakes," but too few have heard about
the role government played in the scandal. That of course
should come as no surprise. Nor should it come as a surprise
there aren't calls in Congress for a full investigation into
what caused the disaster. Banks, S&Ls and other federally
regulated industries contribute large amounts of cash to the
election campaigns of those who write our *regulatory laws*.
–No need to start poking around there. Economist Hans
Sennholz summed up the S&L debacle this way:

> "The real cause of the disaster is the very financial
> structure that was fashioned by legislators and guided
> by regulators; they together created a cartel that,

like all other monopolistic concoctions, is playing mischief with its victims."

And G. Edward Griffin agrees:

"The Savings and Loan industry is really a cartel *within* a cartel. It could not function without Congress standing by to push unlimited amounts of money into it. And Congress could not do that without the banking cartel called the Federal Reserve System standing by as the "lender of last resort" to create money out of nothing for Congress to borrow. This comfortable arrangement between political scientists and monetary scientists permits Congress to vote for any scheme it wants, regardless of the cost. If politicians tried to raise that money through taxes, they would be thrown out of office. But being able to "borrow" it from the Federal Reserve System...allows them to collect it through the hidden mechanism of inflation, and not one voter in a hundred will complain."

Fast forward to September of 2008 and we arrive at the *biggest and best* financial crisis ever engineered. Predictably, we also arrive at the biggest and best "banker bailout" ever stolen from the pockets of U.S. taxpayers.

Despite massive public opposition, on October 3, 2008, Treasury Secretary Henry Paulson was able to ram a **700 billion** dollar "Troubled Asset Relief Program" through Congress. (Intense pressure from voters had initially defeated efforts to enact the TARP legislation. It seems Paulson overcame that pressure by telling legislators there would be chaos in the streets, and even martial law, if they refused to pass the bill.[7])

Both the crisis and the bailout are still unfolding. *Low* estimates for the final cost run well over **5 TRILLION** dollars. To give you an idea of how much money that is, if you spent 1 million dollars *per day*, it would take you nearly 14,000 years to reach $5 trillion...

So far we've witnessed how the bailout game is played. We've seen failure and fraud rewarded, accountability avoided, and the enormous costs heaped onto the backs of the American people. Would you believe me if I said everything outlined until now is only a small part of the game? It's true. ...And in the next few chapters we're going to highlight the real objectives of *the system* and the unspeakable costs of allowing it to survive.

---

7 Representative Brad Sherman's speech before the House of Representatives: *"Many of us were told in private conversations that if we voted against this bill on Monday that the sky would fall, the market would drop two or three thousand points the first day, another couple of thousand the second day, and a few members were even told that there would be martial law in America if we voted no."* Senator James Inhofe, in a radio interview with Tulsa Oklahoma's 1170 KFAQ, named Paulson specifically as the source of the "martial law" comment.

CHAPTER 4
Dreaming of a New World Order

David Rockefeller at a Bilderberg Group meeting in June of 1991: "We are grateful to The Washington Post, The New York Times, Time Magazine and other great publications whose directors have attended our meetings and respected their promises of discretion for almost forty years. It would have been impossible for us to develop our plan for the world if we had been subject to the bright lights of publicity during those years. But, **the world is now much more sophisticated and prepared to march towards a world government. The supranational sovereignty of an _intellectual elite_ and _world bankers_ is surely preferable to the national auto-determination practiced in past centuries.**"[8]

Translation: A world government, created and controlled, by an UNELECTED _"intellectual elite and world bankers."_

---

8   There is some controversy surrounding the accuracy of this quote. (There are rumors of a leaked transcript from the private Bilderberg meeting and even of an audio recording…as of this writing, I have not been able to track down either.) That said, to my knowledge the quote has never been publicly denied and it mirrors exactly the ideology expressed in the actions of the Bilderberg elite. The reader can decide if the quote, in any way, conflicts with what is easily established.

The Federal Reserve System, working in concert with our government, is the very ground on which the bailout game is played. Acting as "lender of last resort," the Fed not only props up our fraudulent banking system, it enables the inevitable losses to be shifted from the cartel to the American people. Far from protecting the public, it has overseen a transfer of wealth that, if fully calculated, would total many **trillions** of dollars. It is easy to understand how this empowers those who profit from the system, and weakens those victimized by it.

But the game is much larger than what we've seen to this point. The Federal Reserve System has expanded its operations. Through a complex system of loans, grants, and subsidies, it is now acting as "lender of last resort" to the entire world. The numbers in this expanded game are much bigger and the ultimate price we're to pay is terrifying.

At this point we're hemorrhaging more than money; we're being bled of our strength as a nation. And that is precisely the plan. With the creation of the World Bank and the International Monetary Fund (IMF) in 1944, the prospect of a *"world government"* ruled by an *"intellectual elite and world bankers"* became a very real possibility. Now, over 60 years later, it is fast becoming a reality.

The World Bank and the IMF

The World Bank and IMF were created at a meeting known as the Bretton Woods Conference. The *stated* aims of these two new international agencies were, as one would expect, quite noble.

The World Bank was established to make loans to war-torn or underdeveloped nations. These loans, it was said, would help the borrowing nations develop their economies and raise living standards. Unfortunately, the loans did little more than help *"notoriously corrupt regimes"* run up enormous debts. Despite its claims, the World Bank's policies looked more like those of *"an institution obsessed with lending, no matter to whom, and no matter with what results...the poor remained mired in poverty...their governing elites amassed obscene fortunes."*[9] (We'll cover this in more detail later in the chapter.)

The IMF was established to *"promote monetary cooperation"* between nations by *"maintaining fixed exchange rates between their currencies."* Sounds great, but the way the IMF would achieve this goal was anything but "great."

At the time, currency exchange rates were determined by how much gold a particular currency could buy on the open market. As a very simple example, imagine 1 U.S. dollar can purchase 1 ounce of gold whereas it takes 2 Canadian dollars to purchase an ounce of gold. Using this information, it's easy to determine the *exchange rate* for U.S. and Canadian currency. (1 U.S. dollar is worth 2 Canadian dollars in this example.) Politicians and bankers hated this method of determining exchange rates because they couldn't easily manipulate it.

To illustrate, assume Canada wants to start "creating lots of money out of nothing" (inflating their currency). As they

---

9   A Game as Old as Empire (first edition), page 158

create more Canadian dollars they drive down the purchasing power of those Canadian dollars. That loss of purchasing power will soon show up in the gold market. Suddenly, it takes 3 Canadian dollars to purchase an ounce of gold, then before long it takes 4 or more. As gold reveals the weakness in the Canadian currency, Canada will suffer the legitimate consequences of its actions. (The value of its currency will drop in world markets and anyone "buying" with Canadian dollars will receive less in exchange for them.)

Speaking on the goal of the IMF, G. Edward Griffin puts it this way:

> "...It was to terminate the use of gold as the basis of international currency exchange and replace it with a politically manipulated paper standard. ...it was to allow governments to escape the discipline of gold so they could create money out of nothing without paying the penalty of having their currencies drop in value on world markets."

Before we proceed, a little background on the two individuals who brought us the World Bank and IMF is in order. One was the well-known Fabian Socialist from England, John Maynard Keynes and the other was Assistant Secretary of the U.S. Treasury Department, Harry Dexter White. An investigation by the United States Senate (Internal Security Subcommittee) had this to say of Assistant Secretary White:

> "The concentration of Communist sympathizers in the Treasury Department, and particularly the Division of Monetary Research, is now a matter of record...**White, Coe**, (Emphasis added) Glasser,

Kaplan, and Perlo were all identified as participants in the Communist conspiracy ..."

Regarding the Fabian socialists, Griffin explains:

"The Fabians were an elite group of intellectuals who formed a semi-secret society for the purpose of bringing socialism to the world. Whereas Communists wanted to establish socialism quickly through violence and revolution, the Fabians preferred to do it slowly through propaganda and legislation. The word socialism was not to be used. Instead, they would speak of the benefits for the people such as welfare, medical care, higher wages, and better working conditions. In this way, they planned to accomplish their objective without bloodshed and even without serious opposition."

Although the Communists and Fabians disagreed on how to establish global socialism, they were willing to work with each other to accomplish their goal. Harry Dexter White, while simultaneously working for a Communist espionage ring, became the United States' first Executive Director for the IMF, and Virginius Frank Coe, also a member of the same Communist espionage ring, became the first Secretary of the IMF. Working together, the Fabians and Communists hoped to create a mechanism by which they could establish a one-world central bank, issue a global *fiat currency* and gain control of all the economies of the world.[10]

---

10 In chapter 6, we'll cover the term "fiat currency" in greater detail. For now, this is all you need to know: Those who are given "the exclusive right" to create fiat currency gain nearly absolute power over the people who are forced to use it.

But before any of this could happen, the United States would have to be brought to its knees economically. (A strong U.S. would never willingly allow itself to be *absorbed* into the "collective whole" of a one-world government.) The World Bank would be a useful tool for this purpose.

The Communists especially liked the idea of transferring wealth out of the U.S. and other industrialized nations (in the form of World Bank loans, grants, subsidies, etc.) into the hands of the underdeveloped nations where *cooperative leaders* held power. (*Leaders* who were happy to impose World Bank and IMF policies in exchange for cash... cash that those *leaders* promptly sent, by the millions and sometimes BILLIONS, to their private offshore bank accounts.)

Although John Maynard Keynes wanted the IMF to issue its own global fiat currency, he knew he couldn't achieve that goal immediately. To convince other nations to participate, the IMF currency would need some form of gold backing. At the time, foreigners could still redeem their U.S. dollars in gold and that made it the perfect choice. So, as a "starting point," the IMF chose the U.S. dollar to be its global monetary unit. The issue of eliminating its gold backing could be dealt with later. Keynes explains:

> "I felt that the leading central banks would never voluntarily relinquish the then existing forms of the gold standard...The only practical hope lay, therefore, in a gradual evolution in the forms of a managed world currency, taking the existing gold standard as a starting point."

The IMF plan for a global fiat currency lunged forward in 1970 with the creation of a new IMF monetary unit called the SDR. (Special Drawing Right.) Although heralded as "paper gold," the SDR has no relation to gold whatsoever. In short, an SDR is nothing more than another way to create money out of nothing and guarantee that somebody else will "pay the price" if things go badly. Here is a brief explanation of how it works. Although the IMF has many member nations, we'll use the United States in this example:

First, the IMF calls on the United States to issue some "credits." These credits aren't really money; they are simply a promise to produce money if necessary. Again we can use a gambling analogy to explain this further. If you're a well-known high roller and you go to a casino, it's common to be given a line of "credit" from the casino. Basically, the casino is saying, "We know you're good for this money so you just go ahead and play and have a good time...if you lose, we'll settle up later." The casino is putting up the money that you get to play with (in the form of credit) knowing that, if you lose, you'll pay that money back. With IMF credits we have essentially the same thing, only in this case it's the United States putting up the "credit" that the IMF gets to gamble with. When the IMF gambles and loses (makes bad loans), the U.S. citizen gets to pick up the tab.

A simple example: The United States issues a "credit" of $1 billion to the IMF. The IMF considers that credit a $1 billion asset (even though it hasn't received a penny, let alone a billion dollars). The IMF then uses that *asset* to create 1 billion worth of SDRs (out of thin air) and *loans* that to another country. If the loan goes bad (if the SDRs created out of thin air aren't repaid), you and I are called on to pay the billion dollar debt.

Although SDRs were a huge leap forward toward creating a global fiat currency, in 1970 the US dollar was still redeemable in gold at a price of $35 per ounce. That caused a problem. Since the IMF used the dollar as its primary currency, and since the dollar was still backed by gold, the amount of money the IMF could issue (create out of nothing) was limited.[11] Griffin explains:

> "If the IMF were to function as a true world central bank with *unlimited* issue, the dollar had to be broken away from its gold backing as a first step toward replacing it completely with...an SDR or something else equally free from restraint.
>
> On August 15, 1971, President Nixon signed an executive order declaring that the United States would no longer redeem its paper dollars for gold. So ended the first phase of the IMF's metamorphosis. It was not yet a true central bank...It had to depend

---

11 We'll cover how "gold backing" limits the amount of money that can be created in chapter six. For now, consider this a simple example: I decide that I want to "create" a new currency. So, I begin printing a new monetary unit that I call a "JOSEPH." To get people to accept my new "JOSEPHS" as payment for their products and services, I explain that each JOSEPH is 100% backed by gold. That means a person who has "JOSEPHS" can exchange them for gold at any time. To keep things easy, we'll say that each JOSEPH can be exchanged for one ounce of gold. If I (the creator of the new "JOSEPH" currency) have only 1,000 ounces of gold (and if I intend to honor my guarantee of 100% gold backing) I am limited to creating 1,000 JOSEPHS. (Clearly, if I have only 1,000 ounces of gold and I create 2,000 JOSEPHS, my entire gold supply would be drained after redeeming only half of the JOSEPHS that I've created... those who did not redeem their JOSEPHS before I ran out of gold would be stuck holding worthless paper.)

on the central banks of its member nations to provide cash and so-called credits; but since these banks, themselves, could create as much money as they wished from now on, there would be no limit."

If you remember, the IMF was established to "promote monetary cooperation between nations" by "maintaining fixed exchange rates between their currencies." With the dollar no longer backed by gold, a ready standard for measuring currency values no longer existed. Not a problem; the IMF simply changed its focus. It would now be in charge of "overcoming trade deficits."

Trade Deficits

We hear a lot about trade deficits, but many don't understand what the term means. To put it in the simplest terms, we'll drop the term "trade" and simply focus on the word "deficit." A deficit is what you get when you spend more money than you make. "Going in the hole" is a common term recognized by most people. If you earn $3,000 this month, but you spend $4,000, you will "go in the hole" $1,000. That $1,000 represents the deficit (the amount of money) between what you earned and what you spent.

A "trade" deficit is very similar. If we say the United States trade deficit is 1 billion dollars per day, it means the United States is spending 1 billion dollars per day more than it's earning. More specifically, the United States is spending $1 billion more per day purchasing products and services from other countries than other countries are spending purchasing products and services from the United States.

Whether you're a person spending more than you earn or a nation spending more than you earn, at some point you're going to run into problems.

> "...the process cannot be sustained unless: (1) earnings are increased; (2) money is taken out of savings; (3) assets are sold; (4) money is counterfeited; or (5) money is borrowed. Unless one of these occurs, the individual or the country has no choice but decrease spending."

(1) Clearly, the best option is to earn more money. Other than decreasing spending, increasing revenue is the only way a nation can actually fix the imbalance.

(2) Taking money out of savings is an option, but only if savings exist. Few nations have any savings at all. Besides, savings are a temporary fix for making up shortfalls in revenue. They do not fix the problem and eventually savings run out.

(3) Selling assets? Sure, but that doesn't fix the problem either. And, there are only so many assets to sell. Like savings, you'll eventually run out.

(4) The counterfeiting option (creating new money out of thin air to cover the deficit). This option only works if you're in the unique position of having your nation's currency accepted as the *world's reserve currency*. The United States dollar has enjoyed the advantages of this unique position for some time now, but it is also on the verge of suffering the unique consequences.

In short: Because the rest of the world has been willing to "buy" U.S. dollars (stockpiling them so they can more easily trade with other nations), the Federal Reserve has been able to create boatloads of money without causing **massive** price inflation in America. But America's free ride is showing signs of coming to an end. Along with its value, the dollar's international status has been dropping steadily against other currencies. This decline not only decreases the likelihood other countries will continue buying dollars as fast as the Federal Reserve can create them; it increases the threat of a massive international move away from the dollar. If that happens, trillions of dollars (currently held in foreign banks) will flood into the U.S. economy and America will experience price inflation unlike anything seen in its recent history.

Again, counterfeiting only applies to the U.S. (and might not apply for much longer) so let's move now to the final option all countries have for overcoming their trade deficits.

(5) The fifth and final option is borrowing. Depending on how "borrowed funds" are spent, this could be the worst option of all. If a country is already spending more than it earns, it makes little sense to further strain its financial resources by piling on debt and interest payments. But this final option is exactly where the IMF has positioned itself to *help* struggling nations overcome their trade deficits. The IMF, supposedly, now stands ready to *loan* these nations into prosperity.

> "These loans do not go into private enterprise where they have a chance of being turned for a profit. They go into state-owned and state-operated industries which are constipated by bureaucracy and poisoned

by corruption. Doomed to economic failure from the start, they consume the loans with no possibility of repayment. Even the interest quickly becomes too much to handle. Which means the IMF must fall back to the "reserves," back to the "assets," back to the "credits," and eventually back to the taxpayers to bail them out.

"Whereas the International Monetary Fund is evolving into a world central bank which eventually will issue a world currency based on nothing, its sister organization, the World Bank, has become its lending agency."

In reality, the World Bank was seen by its founders as a way to covertly bring about social and political change. G. Edward Griffin is more direct: *"The change it was designed to bring about was the building of world socialism, and that is exactly what it is accomplishing today."*

Since the socialist agenda is always wrapped in appealing paper, we might be wise to peel back the wrapping and take a look inside. For now, let's look at some of the governments the World Bank has been kind enough to finance in exchange for *help* with its agenda.

Financing Corruption and Despotism

In Zimbabwe, Uganda, Tanzania and Ethiopia, we find some disturbing examples of World Bank *help*. One could effectively argue the regimes in these nations, sponsored by the World Bank, have been less than *humanitarian* in their approach to *improving the conditions* of their people.

Mass detentions, torture and murder, mass confiscations of property; human beings forced off their land, loaded onto trucks, and "resettled" into compounds where they could be watched and controlled. It looks a lot more like tyranny when you rip away the "utopia wrapping."

In Laos, Syria, Indonesia, China and the former Soviet Union, we see more of the same. Political opposition jailed, political opposition massacred, millions uprooted from their homelands, students murdered and religious leaders imprisoned, civilians slaughtered; yet those responsible have been given billions by the World Bank.

> "The brutalities of these countries are all in a day's work for serious socialists who view them as merely unfortunate necessities for the building of their utopia....George Bernard Shaw, one of the early leaders of the Fabian Socialist movement expressed it this way:
>
>> 'Under Socialism, you would not be allowed to be poor. You would be forcibly fed, clothed, lodged, taught, and employed whether you liked it or not. If it were discovered that you had not the character and industry enough to be worth all this trouble, you might possibly be executed in a kindly manner; but whilst you were *permitted to live,* you would have to live well.'" (Emphasis added.)

Getting Rich along the way

Some seek political control not for "the good of others," but for their own personal benefit. In fact, a look at history reveals this is *most often* the case. Become a high-ranking official or *leader* of a country and odds are you're going to enjoy a privileged life of wealth and power. When billions upon billions (upon billions) of dollars are being tossed around, it's naive to think the elites in charge of those billions aren't going to live by a different set of rules. Graham Hancock, in his book *Lords of Poverty*, has this to say about the international aid "industry:"

> "Corrupt Ministers of Finance and dictatorial Presidents from Asia, Africa, and Latin America are tripping over their own expensive footwear in their unseemly haste...For such people, money has probably never been easier to obtain than it is today; with no complicated projects to administer and no messy accounts to keep, the venal, the cruel and the ugly are laughing literally all the way to the bank.... All they have to do—amazing but true—is screw the poor, and they've already had plenty of practice at that."

Griffin adds:

> "While Nigeria and Argentina are drowning in debt, billions from the World Bank have gone into building lavish new capital cities to house government agencies and the ruling elite. In Zaire, Mexico, and the Philippines, political leaders became billionaires while receiving World Bank Loans on behalf of their nations. In the Central African Republic, IMF and World Bank loans were used to stage a coronation for its emperor. ...The record of corruption and waste is endless."

As bad as the story has been to this point, it wouldn't be complete without taking a look at the *national prosperity* that borrowing nations have enjoyed after receiving IMF/World Bank *help*. In the interest of time, we'll cover just a few examples.

Tanzania, prior to receiving loans from the World Bank, could feed its own population and was experiencing economic growth. In fact, Tanzania (in 1966) not only fed its own people, its main export was food to other nations. $3 billion in loans later, its farms and industries were *nationalized* and every business converted into a government agency. Under the new system, there was no longer enough food to feed the population, nor was there enough money to pay for the food that now had to be imported. That shortfall in funds was of course made up with even more loans and foreign *aid*. The country is now hopelessly mired in debt with no way of getting out.

Argentina went from having one of the highest standards of living in all of Latin America to being an absolute debt-ridden basket case. Following massive loans and the implementation of IMF demands, the gross national product went into a nose dive, manufacturing fell to less than half capacity, bankruptcy, unemployment and welfare soared, and the enormous increase in the nation's money supply drove inflation to 1 MILLION percent!! (1,000,000%) From a prosperous people to paupers; many wonder if the predictably disastrous policies used to blow out thriving economies are *by accident* or *by design*.

When oil was discovered in Mexico, its politicians immediately took the promise of prosperity to the bank.

With borrowed billions, they funded the creation of chemical plants, railroads, Petroleos Mexicanos (PEMEX) and other industrial projects. However, having no knowledge of how to run these newly created entities as legitimate businesses, they lost money. Rather than correct the underlying economic imbalances that, in turn, led to a series of related economic consequences for the nation, the government borrowed *more* money and even began creating its own fiat currency. When that proved ineffective, next came price controls and then a doubling of the minimum wage. By 1982 the Mexican Peso was so weak it was nearly worthless. Keep in mind, all of this was going on while oil prices and production were high. When oil prices started to decrease, it only made matters worse.

By 1995, Mexican loans were in danger of default and U.S. citizens (courtesy of congress) were on the hook for some $30 billion. Griffin continues:

> "Although this loan was eventually repaid, the money to do so was extracted from the Mexican people through another round of massive inflation, which plunged their standard of living even lower...
>
> Thus, the saga continues. After pouring billions of dollars into underdeveloped countries around the globe, no development has taken place. In fact, we have seen just the opposite. Most countries are worse off than before the *Saviors of the World* got to them.
>
> (The IMF and World Bank have) ...become the engine for transferring wealth from the industrialized

nations to the underdeveloped countries. While this has lowered the economic level of the donating countries, it has not raised the level of the recipients. The money has simply disappeared down the drain of political corruption and waste."

When people with obscene amounts of money and power provide insight into how they operate, we'd be well advised to pay attention. In 1838, Amschel Mayer Rothschild is quoted as saying, *"Permit me to issue and control the money of a nation, and I care not who makes its laws."* In an earlier statement, Nathan Mayer Rothschild is quoted: *"I care not what puppet is placed upon the throne of England to rule the Empire... The man who controls Britain's money supply controls the British Empire, and I control the British money supply."*

Those conspiring to bring us a *"world government"* ruled by an *"intellectual elite and world bankers"* are not playing games. They've worked hard to perfect and implement their strategy of economic conquest. They've proven their ability to seize control of nations large and small (even far-flung empires). They certainly haven't come all this way for nothing. This brings us to:

The IMF/World Bank could not function without a steady flow of American dollars and those American dollars *would not* flow without the Fed. The Fed is a tool of our sworn enemies, those hostile to the existence of free and independent nations (and people) everywhere. The time for talk has long since passed. The time for Congress to abolish the Federal Reserve System and reestablish a legitimate monetary system is now.

Summary

An unelected cabal of *"intellectual elite and world bankers"* is using the Federal Reserve System to create a "world government" that they will control. By bringing us to our knees economically, they can more easily erase our borders, erase our Constitution and Bill of Rights...erase *America* as we know it.

But it isn't just America that will suffer; every nation on the face of this planet (regardless of *"what puppet is placed upon"* each regional throne) will be at the mercy of a handful of men if their vision of world government succeeds. By abolishing the Fed, we will wrench from their hands one of the most powerful weapons they possess.

In the next chapter, we'll go deeper into who the players in this game are and how they've already begun "consolidating" the world into more easily managed regions.

CHAPTER 5
Building a New World Order

So far we've covered the game called "bailout" in some detail. We've shown how those engaged in "reckless banking" can turn the natural consequences of their actions into enormous profits. We've shown how you and I are ultimately the ones who provide those profits. But there is another kind of profit being gained at our expense.

By weakening us financially, those who control our monetary system are incrementally increasing their leverage. A wealthy, proud, and independent nation would never willingly surrender its sovereignty and ability to choose its own destiny. An economically devastated nation, chaotic and struggling to maintain social order, is another story altogether. Such a nation would be far more willing to accept *help* from a global body like the United Nations or IMF/ World Bank, regardless of the strings attached. And *THAT is* the ultimate "profit" being sought in this game. The real prize is *control*.

In nation after nation, these "economic warriors" make use of politicians who are willing to bury their citizens in debt. Out of that crushing debt, and the subsequent need for an endless supply of new loans, they slowly gain control.

"Since this game results in a hemorrhage of wealth from the industrialized nations, their economies are doomed to be brought down further and further... The result will be a severe lowering of their living standards and their demise as independent nations. ...The underdeveloped nations, on the other hand, are *not* being raised up. What *is* happening to them is that their political leaders are becoming addicted to the IMF cash flow and will be unable to break the habit. ...They are becoming mere components in the system of world socialism...Their leaders are being groomed to become potentates in a new, high-tech feudalism, paying homage to their lords...And they are eager to do it in return for privilege and power within the *New World Order*."

The Role of the CFR

The Council on Foreign Relations (CFR) is perhaps the most visible cog in the New World Order machine. CFR members have openly and unapologetically called for the weakening of our economic and political sovereignty as a way to establish world government. Admiral Chester Ward, a long time CFR member who later became a harsh critic, summed up the prevailing goal of the CFR this way: "*...the submergence of U.S. sovereignty and national independence into an all-powerful one-world government.*"

Admiral Ward's assertion is backed by countless references. Consider this a short list. (All emphases added.)

"...the house of world order will have to be built from the bottom up rather than from the top down...

an end run around national sovereignty, **eroding it piece by piece**, will accomplish much more than the old-fashioned frontal assault." –CFR member Richard Gardner in an article published in the CFR journal *Foreign Affairs*.

"Some dilution or leveling off of the sovereignty system as it prevails in the world today must take place ... to the immediate disadvantage of those nations which now possess the preponderance of power...**The United States must be prepared to make sacrifices...in setting up a world politico-economic order**." –CFR member Foster Dulles, later appointed Secretary of State by CFR member Dwight Eisenhower.

"...some international cooperation has already been achieved, but further progress will require greater American sacrifices. More intensive efforts to shape a **new world monetary structure** will have to be undertaken with some consequent risk to the present relatively favorable American position." –CFR member and National Security Adviser Zbigniew Brzesinski.

"The standard of living for the average American has to decline. ...I don't think you can escape that." –CFR member and former Chairman of the Federal Reserve, Paul Volcker.

"We shall have world government, whether or not we like it. The question is only whether world government will be achieved by consent or by conquest." –CFR member James Paul Warburg (son of Federal Reserve co-founder Paul Warburg) in a statement before the U.S. Senate Committee on Foreign Relations.

It's important to know, wherever you find people in positions of power, you find the CFR. Griffin explains:

> "...**almost all** of America's leadership has come from this small group. That includes presidents and their advisors, cabinet members, ambassadors, board members of the Federal Reserve System, directors of the largest banks and investment houses, presidents of universities, and heads of metropolitan newspapers, news services, and TV networks."

Before moving on, we should also briefly mention the Trilateral Commission. Created by David Rockefeller in 1973, the Trilateral Commission has been called the *little brother* of the CFR and it was established (no surprise here) to further assist in the creation of global government.

However, unlike the CFR, the Trilateral Commission was specifically focused on bringing Pacific Asia into the global government equation. It has succeeded. Starting with Japan in 1973, the Pacific Asian branch now consists of members from Japan, South Korea, Indonesia, Malaysia, the Philippines, Singapore, Thailand, China, Hong Kong and Taiwan, as well as Australia and New Zealand.

Former presidential candidate Barry Goldwater called the Trilateral Commission *"David Rockefeller's newest cabal,"* and in speaking of its aims he said, *"It is intended to be the vehicle for multinational consolidation of the commercial and banking interests by seizing control of the political government of the United States."*

When it comes to how the New World Order crowd ultimately plans to complete the creation of their one-world government, G. Edward Griffin cuts right to the chase:

> "The objective is to draw the United States, Mexico, Canada, Japan, and Western Europe into political and economic union. Under slogans such as free trade and environmental protection, each nation is to surrender its sovereignty "piece by piece" until a full-blown regional government emerges from the process. ... Once that has happened, it will be a relatively simple step to merge the regional governments into global government. That is the reality behind the so-called trade treaties within the European Union (EU), the North American Free Trade Agreement (NAFTA), the Asia-Pacific Economic Cooperation agreement (APEC), and the General Agreement on Tariffs and Trade (GATT)."

Expanding on Griffin's assertion, the EU (European Union) provides a perfect example. What we now call the EU began as a simple trade agreement in 1951 between six European countries. That agreement was called *The European Coal and Steel Community* and it established a "free trade area" where coal and steel could be bought and sold without import/export duties. (In that very *limited* sense, the agreement "erased the borders" between those member nations.)

But in 1957, a new agreement was signed and the concept of *cooperation* among member nations was greatly expanded.

The new agreement was called the *European Economic Community* and its ultimate aim was the economic and eventual political merger of its member nations. (Policies on labor, social welfare, agriculture, transportation, foreign trade, etc. were to be "harmonized.")

In 1992, the word "economic" was dropped and the organization became known as simply the *European Community*. And finally, in 1993, the European Community became the *European Union*.

What began as a simple trade agreement has now morphed into a supranational government entity that is more powerful than its member nations (of which there are now 27). These 27 member nations have already lost a great deal of control over their own countries, but the EU powerbrokers have far bigger things in mind. Look no further than a recently proposed European *Justice System* for proof of that. Under *"Corpus Juris"* the citizens of member nations would have:

- No right to a trial by jury. The accused would go before a state appointed judge to be pronounced guilty or innocent.

- No right to Habeas Corpus. Anyone declared a **suspect** can be arrested without charges and the suspect would have no right to challenge the legitimacy of their detention. The initial limit for how long the state could keep "a suspect" without presenting evidence was set to 6 months, however that term can be extended AND there is...

- No protection against double jeopardy. Conceivably the state can continue arresting and trying "a suspect" for the same crime until it secures a conviction.

- No presumption of innocence. Rather than the state having to prove its case "beyond a reasonable doubt," suspects are automatically presumed guilty. (Even if you were fortunate enough to convince a judge that his comrades were wrong, you're right back to being potentially brought up on the same charge again.)

That these provisions were even put forward with a straight face provides some insight into the *kind* of "New World Order" our masters intend to build. For the elites looking to stifle and punish all dissent against them, this type of world-wide system would be a utopia. For all others, it would be an inescapable global Hell. (Sadly, many of these OLD concepts of *justice* have already found a home in the United States. It looks as if the intellectual elite driving U.S. policy have outperformed the EU bureaucrats in this regard.)[12]

Again, the EU perfectly illustrates how the framework for global government is being put in place. Nations are convinced to sign on to "trade agreements" that, in effect, give a newly created "supranational" government entity control

---

12 Many were shocked by the brazen violations of basic Constitutional principles under the administration of G.W. Bush. However, those who hoped "Constitutional scholar" Barack Obama would return the U.S. to sanity were undoubtedly amazed when he, in May of 2009, proposed a brand new unconstitutional policy of his own called "preventive detention." Under this new policy, the Federal Government asserts the right to imprison you, indefinitely, based on ZERO evidence of any crime whatsoever. That is, they can put you in a cage not because you committed a crime, not because they believe you "conspired" or attempted to commit a crime, but because they think you might decide to commit a crime in the future! (Good luck proving your innocence against that charge.)

over them. Once a handful of these new entities are in place (A European Union, North American Union, Asia-Pacific Union, etc.), merging those supranational governments into a one-world government will be a relatively simple task. (Whether or not they are ever *officially* merged is irrelevant. In the end, a tiny group of elite will be in complete control, and that is the ultimate aim.)

Enough on the "final play" in this game; let's return now to the transfer of wealth that is helping set it up.

Panama

When Panama fell behind on its bank loans, the major banking interests that stood to lose money had a *brilliant* idea. Chase Manhattan Bank, First National of Chicago, Citibank (and a handful of others) went to Washington and pitched their solution. It was this: The Panama Canal, built at a tremendous cost in American dollars and American lives, would be given to the Panamanian government. The Panamanian government could then use the hundreds of millions in annual revenue generated by the canal to pay back its loans.

Many in the U.S. strongly opposed this giveaway, but in the end Congress dutifully served its real masters. Once again, the politically well-connected and powerful insiders got their way. Regardless of where you stand on the issue of giving the canal to the Panamanian government, this fact remains: The citizens of America, yet again, bailed out the banks. (Hundreds of millions in annual revenue generated by the canal were given away and that lost revenue, ever since, has been made up in one of two ways: taxes or inflation.)

Mexico

In 1982, Mexico announced it would have to halt payments on its $85 billion ($85,000,000,000.00) in debt. But not to worry, the Federal Reserve was standing by to *save the day!* $4.5 billion worth of new loans were arranged with $2.7 billion "created out of nothing" by the Federal Reserve itself. The commercial banks *agreed to accept* "interest only" payments for a couple years and, as a result of the new infusion of cash, the multi-million dollar loan payments resumed. Of course, none of this fixed the underlying problems so, a few years later, Mexico was again behind on its payments. This time the banks agreed to postpone payments on $29 billion and issued $20 billion in *new* loans to replace/pay off some older debts. The game continued.

Can you guess what happens next? Mexico announces it cannot make payments on its debt and the Federal Reserve comes to the rescue. (Surprised?) This time, the head of the Federal Reserve, Paul Volcker, met with Mexico's finance minister and agreed to a "currency swap" of over half a billion dollars to help Mexico get past its upcoming election. Specifically, the United States traded Mexico $600 million US dollars for 600 million essentially worthless Mexican Pesos. Mexico agreed to redeem the Pesos for US dollars at a later date, but could anyone reasonably believe that would happen? Griffin adds:

"The importance of this loan was neither its size nor even the question of repayment. It was the manner in which it was made. First, it was made by the Federal Reserve *directly*, acting as a central bank for Mexico, not the U.S.; and secondly, it was done almost in total secrecy."

When the currency swap failed to solve the problem, a new and even more imaginative move was implemented in 1988: a *debt swap*. What follows would actually be funny if it wasn't so irritating. First, a brief explanation:

The United States government offers Treasury bonds that pay no interest while you hold them, but when the bonds "mature" (when the day arrives that you're allowed to cash them in) they are worth much more than their original cost. So, for instance, imagine you purchased one of these Treasury bonds in the amount of $10,000. When the bond matures (say 20 years later) the government will owe you $70,000. Technically, this kind of bond is called a "zero-coupon" bond. ...With that brief explanation out of the way, here is how the "debt swap" with Mexico worked.

Using $492 million dollars, Mexico purchased U.S. Treasury bonds that, on maturity 20 years later, were guaranteed to pay $3.7 billion. Mexico then approached the banks that were holding a fortune in essentially worthless Mexican bonds (bonds that had no chance of being paid by Mexico) with the following offer: "We will trade you the worthless bonds you're now holding for NEW bonds that have this $3.7 billion in U.S. securities backing them as collateral... how does a ratio of 1.4 to 1 sound?"

As a very simple example, imagine one bank was holding $140 million in Mexican bonds. What Mexico was saying is this: *"If you tear up that $140 million debt that we owe you, we'll give you (in exchange) $100 million in new bonds that are backed by these U.S. bonds we now own."* Of course the banks were eager to swap old worthless Mexican bonds for new "U.S. guaranteed bonds." It reduced the bank's interest income some, but in the long run it *guaranteed* a fortune would be made. –Pretty clever, huh?

Now for the fun part: The $492 million that Mexico used to purchase the U.S. bonds came mainly from the IMF. In turn, that means *our government* put up the lion's share of the money used to buy the bonds in the first place. It essentially went half a billion deeper in debt and guaranteed to pay $3.7 **billion** 20 years later, all so Mexico could keep making payments to the banks. But that didn't fix the problem either. Griffin continues:

> "The following year, Secretary of State, James Baker (CFR), and Treasury Secretary, Nicholas Brady (CFR), flew to Mexico to work out a new debt agreement that would begin to phase in the IMF as final guarantor. The IMF gave Mexico a new loan of $3.5 billion (later increased to $7.5 billion), the World Bank gave another $1.5 billion, and the banks reduced their previous loan values by about a third. The private banks were quite willing to extend new loans and reschedule the old. Why not? Interest payments would now be guaranteed by the taxpayers of the United States and Japan."

Do you see a pattern here? Let's hope so. And following that pattern, what do you think happened after the aforementioned $9 billion in additional loans were given? Do you think that money *fixed the problem*? We'll pick up in December of 1994.

> "At the end of 1994, the game was still going...Once again Mexico could not pay the interest on its loans. On January 11, President Bill Clinton (CFR) urged Congress to approve U.S. guarantees for new loans up to $40 billion. Secretary of the Treasury Robert Rubin (CFR) explained: 'It is the judgment of all, including Chairman Alan Greenspan (CFR), that the probability of the debts being paid (by Mexico) is exceedingly high.' But, while Congress debated the issue, the loan clock was ticking. Payment of $17 billion in Mexican bonds was due within 60 days, and $4 billion of that was due on the first of February! *Who* was going to pay the banks?
>
> This matter could not wait. On January 31, acting independently of Congress, President Clinton announced a bailout package of over $50 billion in loan guarantees to Mexico: $20 billion from the U.S. Exchange Stabilization Fund, $17.8 billion from the IMF, $10 billion from the Bank of International Settlements, and $3 billion from commercial banks."

These stories are so common that to tell them all would become boring. By the early 1980's, Third-World governments owed three quarters of a trillion dollars and dozens of them were behind on their payments. As of this writing, the total debt of developing nations is well over **TWO TRILLION.** Through it all, we find the same game and the same players.

For instance, in 1987 Brazil was in default (again) on over $120 billion in debt. Despite having a fortune pass through its hands, the government was so broke it couldn't even put gas in its police cars. In 1989, President Bush Sr. (CFR) upped the ante by calling for debt *forgiveness* as a solution to the entire Third-World debt problem. (Debt forgiveness sounds very humanitarian, but let's not forget who we're dealing with. Few take the time to look at the strings attached to *debt forgiveness* or contemplate how those strings benefit the ones who are doing the "forgiving.") But returning to Brazil, a little over a decade later, President Bush's son (Bush Jr.) was pushing for another $30 billion IMF loan, backed by US citizens, to *help* Brazil overcome its payment problems.

In 1982, an IMF loan of $2.15 billion was necessary to *help* Argentina make a $2.5 billion payment it owed. Within a year of receiving this help, Argentina was again unable to keep up with its payments. The banks scrambled to arrange new terms, guarantees, and IMF loans. An additional $4.2 billion was loaned to cover interest payments and also provide some political incentives. By 1988, Argentina had again stopped making payments on its loans. To make a long story short, by 2002 the IMF had bailed out Argentina to the tune of an *additional* $48 **billion**.

> "It would be counterproductive to cover the same sordid story as it has unfolded in each country. Suffice to say that the identical game has been played with teams from Bolivia, Peru, Venezuela, Costa Rica, Morocco, the Philippines, the Dominican Republic, and almost every other less-developed country in the world."

The Great Deception

No *world government* would be complete without including Communist China and the former Soviet Union. However, before either of these nations could be merged into the New World Order puzzle, they required a serious image makeover. After all, citizens of the United States, as well as other western governments, would be unlikely to support the transfer of hundreds of billions of dollars to the *totalitarian enemies of freedom*. And as we already know, without the IMF/World Bank mechanism doing its job (transferring billions and acquiring the kind of *cooperation* that only billions of dollars will buy), everything becomes complicated. So maybe those "nasty commies" could be persuaded to drop the open hostility, take a more moderate stance, and reap the financial and ideological rewards of doing so.

> "...the apparent crumbling of Communism has created an acceptable rationale for the industrialized nations to now allow their lifeblood to flow into the veins of their former enemies. It also creates the appearance of global, political "convergence," a condition which CFR theoretician, Richard Cooper, said was necessary before Americans would accept having their own destinies determined by governments other than their own."

Communist China joined the IMF/World Bank in 1980 and by 1987 it was the IMF's second largest borrower. While billions of dollars were being funneled into China (supposedly to help fight poverty, develop natural resources and improve living standards), the Chinese government was busy dumping billions into military development. In other words, China already *had the money*; it simply chose to spend it elsewhere, and IMF/World Bank loans only made it easier for it to do so.

It's kind of odd. Back in the good old days, when government-forced abortions, interference in the free market, land confiscations, slave labor, prisoner organ harvesting, religious persecution, torture, and nearly zero tolerance for freedom of speech were a big deal, China was (at least in the eyes of the West) an absolute pariah. But now that China is one of our "strongest trading partners," all of these things no longer seem to matter. ...This provides some priceless insight into how our governments *choose* our enemies. When it suits them to attack and vilify a nation, they do so with a vengeance. When it suits them to keep quiet, the silence is deafening.

Then there is the former Soviet Union. Can anyone really say where all the Communists went? For nearly a century, there they were; the gravest threat the free world ever faced. Menacing and powerful, they maintained their control over the Russian people with force and violence...a tyrannical cabal that created and controlled the world's **only other superpower;** and then, in the blink of an eye, they all just went away? Nobody wants to rob the West of its proudest moment (its victory over Communism), but doesn't the magic vanishing act of "The Great Red Menace" warrant a little bit of scrutiny?

Was our victory over Communism everything it was cracked up to be, or was it just a ruse? Did the power brokers in Russia all simultaneously experience a profound ideological shift, or was the new term "Social Democrat" a calculated PR move aimed at softening the image of the former Communists and setting the stage for *convergence*?[13]

A few disposable leaders purged from the ranks, a new public image and promising rhetoric, a long awaited "nod" given to the *greater wisdom* of western ways...Surely it would require more than that to convince the world that Communism had fallen. Apparently not.

> "No other changes are required. Socialism remains the economic system of choice and, although lip service may be given to free-market concepts, the economy and all means of production remain under state control. The old communists are now Social Democrats and, without exception, they become the leaders in the new system.
>
> The West rejoices and the money starts to move. ... former Bolsheviks are now hailed by the world as great statesmen who put an end to the Cold War, brought freedom to their people, and helped to forge a New World Order.
>
> When did Communism depart? We are not quite sure. All we know is that one day we opened our newspapers and it was accomplished. Social

---

13 If you'd like to dig a little deeper into this idea of "preparing the U.S. for convergence," Ed Griffin conducted an interesting interview with Norman Dodd (Director of the Reece Committee), which is available online. During his investigation, Dodd was told by the president of the Ford Foundation: *"Mr. Dodd, all of us who have a hand in the making of policies here have had experience either with the OSS* (predecessor of the CIA) *during the war or the European Economic Administration after the war. We've had experience operating under directives...that emanate from the White House...the substance of which is that we shall use our grant-making power to alter life in the United States so that it can be comfortably merged with the Soviet Union."*

Democrats were everywhere. No one could find any Communists. ...Communism was dead. It was not killed by an enemy. It voted itself out of existence. It committed suicide!"

Whether the death of Communism was exaggerated or not is open to debate. What isn't debatable is, since its *death*, the money has flowed like water. And to be clear here, we're not suggesting American banks and corporations weren't making money on *humanitarian loan packages* prior to the announced end of Communism. They certainly were. Just nowhere near as much.

Example: In 1990, just *prior* to "the collapse," President Bush Sr. announced all "sound American corporate investments" in Russia would be 100% insured (for free) with no limit on the amount of coverage. In other words, the bailout game had been expanded to include not just the banks, but other industries as well. It was a promise that, when investments went sour, the taxpayers would pick up the bill. Now, far more people could get in on the lucrative "*bet big, you cannot lose*" government gravy train. Imagine being in charge of an operation like this:

International agencies loan billions of dollars to the "social democrats." Nobody expects the loans to be repaid, but that isn't a problem – the taxpayers will take care of that. In exchange, the social democrats agree to spend the billions purchasing products and services from well-connected American corporations.

In addition to this cozy little arrangement, corporations are offered 100% insurance on anything they invest in

Russian projects. Such lucrative *risk-free* contracts are not awarded based on merit, but on political connections. (Come on, you don't really expect those running the game to let *everyone* in on the easy money, do you?) And finally, when socialist mismanagement drives everything into the dirt, the federal government covers corporate profits and repayment of bank loans by extracting the money from the U.S. citizenry. Chalk up another "win/win" for everyone *but us.*

> "There you have it. The Social Democrats get the goodies; the corporations get the profits, and the banks get the interest on money created out of nothing. You know what the taxpayers get!"

Whether the bailout takes place domestically or internationally, the same individuals (engaged in the deliberate destruction of national sovereignty) are guaranteed to profit. There are the direct and most visible profits (the actual dollars and cents transferred from their rightful owners to the conspirators themselves) and there are the less visible but more significant profits; acquiring the *cooperation* of influential leaders around the globe. The ultimate objective is the creation of an inescapable, financially controlled global tyranny, run by an unelected "intellectual elite and world bankers."

Dr. Carroll Quigley, in his 1300-page book, "Tragedy and Hope," speaks with the authority of an elite insider. In no uncertain terms he exposes the aims of what he refers to as "the network." It is important to note his only real "difference of opinion" is in the network's secretive approach to securing its aims. In his own words:

"I know of the operations of this network because I have studied it for twenty years and was permitted for two years, in the early 1960's, to examine its papers and secret records. I have no aversion to it or to most of its aims and have, for much of my life, been close to it and to many of its instruments...my chief difference of opinion is that it wishes to remain unknown...." [14]

You and I are the targets in this game. As "the network" secretly conspires to manipulate, deceive and literally enslave us all, we have a choice: We can allow them to create *their* government (For the elite, by the elite and of the elite) or we can stop them.

Our problem really isn't that complicated. It's not like trying to reverse the earth's orbit around the sun. These men created

---

14 Tragedy and Hope is a long, dry, and tedious read, but it provides an enormous amount of insight into how the banking elite (in modern history) establish and maintain their power. Discussing the early groundwork (period 1810 – 1850), Quigley says: *"In time they brought into their financial network the provincial banking centers, organized as commercial banks and savings banks, as well as insurance companies, to form all of these into a single financial system on an international scale which manipulated the quantity and flow of money so that they were able to influence, if not control, governments on one side and industries on the other. The men who did this, looking backward toward the period of dynastic monarchy in which they had their own roots, aspired to establish dynasties of international bankers and were at least as successful at this as were many of the dynastic political rulers."* And, discussing the early 1900s, Quigley says: *"In addition to their power over government based on government financing and personal influence, bankers could steer governments in ways they wished them to go by other pressures. Since most government officials felt ignorant of finance, they sought advice from bankers whom they considered to be experts in the field. The history of the last century shows...that the advice given to governments by bankers, like the advice they gave to industrialists, was consistently good for bankers, but was often disastrous for governments, businessmen, and the people generally. Such advice could be enforced, if necessary, by manipulation of exchanges, gold flows, discount rates, and even levels of business activity."*

(and continue to expand) a fraudulent system for their own benefit. It has been built and sustained with human effort; it can be undone just the same. However, one thing we *will* need (to prevent them from simply repackaging their current scheme) is a deeper understanding of *money* and how it is being used against us. We'll cover that in the next chapter.

CHAPTER 6
Honest and Dishonest Money

The *bailout* is one way the elite transfer wealth from our hands to theirs. But it is certainly not the only way, nor is it the most sophisticated. Perhaps the cleverest scam of all is the actual "money" they've created for us to use. Just like the fraudulent mechanisms we've outlined in previous chapters, our *money* has *theft* built right in. By design, it enables wealth to be secretly transferred from those who've *earned* it, to those who create and control it.

Few know the history of money or the many different *forms* money can take. Some forms of money are more prone to fraud than others and our ignorance of this fact works to the advantage of those running the scam. They're more than happy to make us believe only *they* are smart enough to understand the "complex nature of money." Our *monetary policy*, so they say, is best left to the experts; we should just *trust them.* ...Knowing the ultimate goals of those who created our monetary system, we could hardly make a more dangerous mistake.

Defining money

To accurately define what money *is*, we can't simply hold up a US Dollar (or a Russian Ruble, or a Mexican Peso) and say, "This is money." We're better off to start by defining the overall purpose of money. What does money *do*?

In the simplest terms, money enables us to purchase products and services from other people. Using this basic description, we might go on to say: Money *can be* anything that is widely accepted as "payment" for products and services.

Having defined money in this way, it will be easier to explain the different forms of money and why some are far superior to others. However, before we actually get into the different forms of money, it's a good idea to touch on what existed before money. It was known as barter.

Barter

To "barter" basically means to *pay for* something you want with products or services instead of paying for what you want with *money*. As an example, imagine you grow tomatoes and your neighbor grows corn. It's possible to imagine a scenario where you and your neighbor agree to trade 25 pounds of your tomatoes for 25 pounds of his corn. In this scenario, you have each *paid for* what you want with something other than money.

Although barter provides an opportunity to engage in trade with others, this type of trade is far more limited than what we're used to today. To illustrate: What if your neighbor also grows wheat and you need 25 pounds of that too? You offer him another 25 pounds of tomatoes but he declines. (He has no use for any more tomatoes.) Now what do you do?

You might try to find another person who grows wheat and trade with them. Or, you might find somebody who has something that your wheat-growing neighbor wants, trade your tomatoes for that item, and then trade *that item* for the wheat...but clearly none of these options are as convenient as simply trading your neighbor "money" for his wheat, his corn or anything else he might be willing to part with. As you can see in this example, barter was far from ideal.

Even though barter was limited in its usefulness, it played a major role in developing the concept of money. While trading with each other, people realized certain commodities were always in demand. For instance, they eventually discovered corn was so high in demand it could be traded for almost any other product or service. From that point forward, corn took on a value that exceeded its "consumption value." In other words, even though your neighbor already had all the corn *he needed*, he would continue to grow (or acquire) more because he knew the corn would be "accepted as payment" for the products and services of others. The more corn he had, the more purchasing power he had. In this way, many different commodities (corn, wheat, animals, etc.) eventually evolved into reliable forms of *commodity money*.

Now, with that brief explanation of how barter eventually led to "commodity money," let's move on to...

Commodity money

Cows, sheep, corn, wheat; all of these commodities had intrinsic value, were highly "in demand" and, as such, individuals were nearly guaranteed to accept them in trade. For this reason, they became some of the earliest forms of "commodity money." But just as barter was limited, so too was the ability to easily "buy" using indivisible items like a cow. Perishable food items had their limitations as well.

When mankind discovered metal and learned to craft it into tools and weapons, the metals themselves soon took on the role of commodity money (superior to the other commodities in many ways). For starters, metal didn't need to be fed, watered and cleaned up after. And, unlike wheat and corn, you didn't have to worry about metal *going bad*, becoming contaminated with bugs or mold, etc.

Perhaps best of all, metal was easily divisible. Compare the flexibility of purchasing something with a cow versus purchasing something with iron. Assuming a cow is equal in value to 100 pounds of iron, and an item is for sale valued at 10 pounds of iron (or 1/10th of a cow), the individual buying with iron has a distinct advantage; he can easily produce the exact amount of money needed. The same cannot be said for the man trying to purchase the same item using his cow. Sure, he can divide the cow into 10 pieces, but the other 9 wouldn't be worth much for very long.

> "The value of metal ingots was originally determined by weight. Then, as it became customary for the merchants who cast them to stamp the uniform weights on the top, they eventually were valued

simply by counting their number…in this form they became, in effect, primitive but functional coins."

Just as barter led to the concept of commodity *money*, and that led to "metal" becoming the commodity of choice, centuries of experimenting with different kinds of metals produced a clear favorite around the world: Gold. Gold's ability to function as a stable form of money is unmatched. (Silver runs a close second.) When it comes to *"monetary stability,"* the Federal Reserve System has failed miserably compared to gold and silver. But knowing the real aims of those who crafted the system, we shouldn't be surprised.

A common argument against using gold as money today is: "There simply isn't enough of it to go around." Initially, this argument seems reasonable, but taking a closer look reveals its flaws. The truth is "having more gold" is NOT necessary. Whatever the supply of gold is, the market will set values based on that supply. So, if there are only 10 million ounces of gold circulating in an economy, its price (and purchasing power) *per ounce* will be higher than if there are 100 million ounces in circulation. This basic economic truth applies to all money, regardless of the form it takes.

Explaining further:

The more *money* there is circulating in an economy (whether we're talking corn, sheep, gold or paper), the *less* purchasing power that money will have. For example, if we create a community from scratch and give everyone an equal amount of money, (say $10,000 each), prices for products and services within that community will be set based on the available money supply. If instead we give each person

$100,000, the same thing will happen; prices will be set based on the available money supply. If we give them all 10 million dollars, it's no different...the fact everyone has $10 million in our third example will not make any of them any "wealthier" than if they'd each been given only $10,000. More money chasing after the same amount of products and services only bids prices up.

The same thing happens if you start a community with a set money supply and then begin "inflating" the amount of money in existence. So, the first year everyone starts with $10,000 and prices are set according to the total money supply. If the following year, you give another $10,000 to each person (without an increase in newly available products and services), the flood of new money will only bid prices up.

Not long ago, when somebody used the term "inflation," they were referring to the actual act of "inflating/increasing" the money supply. Not today. Now the term is almost always used to describe the *illness* that monetary inflation causes (rising prices). This works out great for those causing the problem. Instead of blaming the real culprits, the public tends to blame the *greedy businessmen* who "keep raising their prices." Well, it isn't an issue of businesses "raising their prices." It's more an issue of the purchasing power of the currency *going down*. As the value of each Dollar is driven down, the number of Dollars it takes to purchase products and services goes up. (The same is true with any currency; Russian Ruble, Mexican Peso, British Pound, etc....dilute the value of the monetary unit and the number of monetary units it takes to purchase products and services will rise.)

I'm getting ahead of the story a little bit, but here is an important point to consider. Imagine for a moment you are an unscrupulous (yet highly intelligent) banker given the legal authority to control the amount of money in the community we just mentioned. Can you think of a way you might be able to use your inflationary power to your advantage? I'll provide an example.

Let's say the community begins with a total *combined* money supply of $50 million. As a banker, you earn money by making loans and charging interest on those loans. So, you begin making loans to the community's inhabitants. Per the current fraudulent banking system, the money for your "loans" is created out of thin air...they cost you nothing. All you've got to do is enter "$100,000" (or whatever the amount may be) into a borrower's checking account and *poof*, you just created the money for the loan.

Unfortunately, by creating this money for the *loan* you also add $100,000 (or whatever the loan amount might be) to the total money supply. You do this over and over and before long, the community's money supply doubles from $50 million to $100 million. Soon, the effects of inflating the money supply start to take their toll; prices are rising, people who actually saved money prior to the inflation are having "purchasing power" stolen from every dollar they earned,[15] and people on

---

15 If it costs $1.00 for a loaf of bread and you have saved $100.00, you might reasonably assume that you've got enough money to buy 100 loaves of bread. However, if due to inflation the cost of bread is driven up to $2.00 per loaf, that $100.00 under your mattress will now only buy *half as much bread*. (The *purchasing power* of your savings has been cut in half.) The end result, regarding what you "have the money to buy," is no different than if somebody stole $50.00 of your savings.

fixed incomes are finding it increasingly difficult to get by. But *you're* doing just fine earning interest on the $50 million in "loans" that you've put into the community.

But why stop there? Being the unscrupulous (yet highly intelligent) banker that you are, you have an idea. You notice real estate prices have doubled from the inflation...some might even call the massive rise in prices a "bubble." You wonder what would happen if you "pop" that bubble. You wonder what would happen if you begin to DECREASE the amount of money in circulation. (But you don't *really* wonder...you know exactly what will happen. The purchasing power of each dollar will begin to rise and as a result, prices will begin to fall.)

Specifically, all the real estate prices that had been "bid up" when there was $100 million in circulation will begin to "correct downward." ...Ah, but the mortgages on all those properties aren't going to "correct downward," no sir. The people who *borrowed* $200,000 from you to buy their home when the bubble was at its peak will still owe you $200,000. This despite the fact, with the money supply tightening, they'd be lucky to sell their home for $150,000. And a couple months from now (caught in the ensuing panic of people trying to sell before their home loses more value) they might not be able to sell it for $100,000!

And that isn't all they've got to worry about. Payments on a $200,000 mortgage were much easier to make when hourly wages in the community were based on a total money supply of $100 million. With only $50 million to go around, it's becoming nearly impossible to earn enough to keep up with (what are now) ridiculously high monthly mortgage payments. And if they are *lucky enough* to stay employed and earn enough to actually pay off their mortgage, their big reward is they'll end up paying double what the home is actually worth. Many will have little choice but give up their homes and try to find another place to live. But is that such a "bad deal" for *you*, the unscrupulous (but highly intelligent) banker who created the money for the loans out of nothing? Probably not.

Let's see: First you *earned* millions in interest payments on "loans" that were made with money created out of thin air. Now you get to seize **real physical assets** (people's homes) because that "money" (keystrokes in a computer) wasn't paid back. ...*And* those millions of dollars you *earned* when people were able to make their payments will now buy twice as much in the economy you just crashed. What a great time to go bargain hunting for new assets, no? Looks like a win/win/win. (Or a lose/lose/lose, depending on which side of the game you're on.)

Would anyone in their right mind want to give a banker (or bankers) this kind of control over their community's money supply? No? Okay, then it certainly doesn't make any sense to give that kind of power to a banker (or bankers) over our **entire nation's** money supply. But that is exactly what our elected officials have done.

> "If the American people ever allow private banks to control the issue of currency, first by inflation, then by deflation, the banks and corporations that will grow up around them will deprive the people of all property until their children wake up homeless on

the continent their fathers conquered." –Attributed to Thomas Jefferson [16]

It doesn't get any more "straight forward" than that.

Returning now to the original point of all this: The argument against gold (that there isn't enough to go around) is fraudulent. The real reason our banker friends don't want an honest monetary system (one that prevents them from "creating money out of nothing") is because of what it would do to their wealth and power. When they insist our "modern economic reality" requires an *elastic* money supply to function properly (*elastic* meaning, they can inflate or deflate as much as they like) they *are* actually telling us the truth. That is, our *modern economic reality* of endless "bubbles" and "bursts," steady inflation, bailouts, inescapable debt and the covert transfer of wealth from our hands to the hands of others really *does* require the system they've created to "function properly." The problem is our *modern economic reality* is unacceptable.

---

16 This quote is often attributed to Thomas Jefferson, but it appears to be a "paraphrase." For instance, the following quote conveys nearly the exact same sentiment, only it's not written in laymen's terms: *"The plethory of circulating medium which raised the prices of everything to several times their ordinary and standard value, in which state...heavy debts were contracted; and the sudden withdrawing too great a proportion of that medium, and reduction of prices far below that standard, constitutes the disease under which we are now laboring...Certainly no nation ever before abandoned to the avarice...of private individuals to regulate, according to their own interests, the quantum of circulating medium for the nation, to inflate, by deluges of paper, the nominal prices of property, and then to buy up that property... having first withdrawn the floating medium which might endanger a competition in purchase. Yet this is what has been done, and will be done, unless stayed by the protecting hand of the legislature. The evil has been produced by the error of their sanction of this ruinous machinery of banks; and justice, wisdom, duty, all require that they should interpose and arrest it before the schemes of plunder and spoliation desolate the country. "* -The works of Thomas Jefferson, Volume 12 (Correspondence and papers 1816 - 1826) in a letter to William C. Rives

It wasn't created to serve our needs; it was created to serve the needs of those who lied it into existence.

On the issue of *needing* an elastic money supply, professor of economics, Murray Rothbard, writes:

> "There is no need whatever for any planned increase in the money supply, for the supply to rise to offset any condition, or to follow any artificial criteria. More money does not supply more capital, is not more productive, does not permit "economic growth.""

The idea of making money *more elastic* isn't new. Even under the discipline of a gold coin monetary system, unscrupulous individuals figured out how to inflate the money supply. By shaving off a small portion of each gold coin that passed through their hands, merchants and kings were able to amass piles of gold shavings which were then melted down and cast into new coins. By now you can surely predict how this affected the economy. Those who created the money would spend it at "full value" and as the newly created coins began to inflate the existing money supply, (driving down the value of existing coins) the number of coins it took to purchase products and services went up.

> "As governments became more brazen in their debasement of the currency, **even to the extent of diluting the gold or silver content,** the population adapted quite well by simply "discounting" the new coins. That is to say, they accepted them at a realistic value, which was lower than what the government had intended. This was, as always, reflected in a general rise in prices…

Governments don't like to be thwarted in their plans to exploit their subjects. So a way had to be found to *force* people to accept these slugs as real money. **This led to the first legal-tender laws.** By royal decree, the "coin of the realm" was declared legal for the settlement of all debts. Anyone who refused it at face value was subject to fine, imprisonment, or, in some cases, even death." (Emphasis added; the paper money we use today has been declared "legal tender" for a reason.)

The King's legal tender laws forced individuals to accept coins that they would have otherwise rejected or, at the very least, discounted heavily. As an example, imagine an economy where all trade is conducted using gold coins. Suddenly, the king decides to start minting coins made of wood. By "royal decree" he demands his new one-ounce wooden coins be accepted at the same rate as one ounce of gold. He declares them *legal tender*. What would the people do?

Well, there is no need to guess. We can simply look at what citizens actually *did do* in response to the first legal tender laws. They began hoarding their truly valuable gold coins. After all, if you were forced to accept junk coins as payment, would you (out of the kindness of your heart) continue making your payments in gold?

The same thing happened in America in the 1960s when silver dimes, quarters and half dollars were replaced with new coins made out of a mixture of copper and nickel. Within months, a good percentage of the silver coins had already been stashed away. Sure, the new "cupronickel" quarters *said* they were worth the same as the old quarters (25 cents) but that didn't mean they really were.

To put it in perspective; a roll of 40 quarters has a stamped face value of $10.00 whether the quarters are made out of silver or the cupronickel of today. However, the *real value* of a roll of silver quarters (based on the weight of the silver alone) is currently over $100.00. So which would you rather have? Would *you* trade a roll of silver quarters for a roll of cupronickel quarters?

Of course, today our rulers have more sophisticated ways to debase our currency. Rather than shaving coins, or replacing solid coins with "plated coins," or intentionally diluting the purity of the gold or silver content, they instead achieve what they want through our modern banking system. Alan Greenspan spoke out against the consequences of this practice in 1966. Ironically, about 20 years later, he was elected **Chairman of the Board of Governors of the Federal Reserve!** *"Even the wisest of men can be corrupted by power and wealth." -Griffin.* Nevertheless, in 1966 Mr. Greenspan laid out the truth in no uncertain terms. He wrote:

> "The abandonment of the gold standard made it possible for the welfare statists to use the banking system as a means to an unlimited expansion of credit...
>
> The law of supply and demand is not to be conned. As the supply of money...increases relative to the supply of tangible assets in the economy, prices must eventually rise. Thus the earnings saved by the productive members of the society lose value...

In the absence of the gold standard, there is no way to protect savings from confiscation through inflation. ...Deficit spending is simply a scheme for the "hidden" confiscation of wealth. Gold stands in the way of this insidious process. It stands as a protector of property rights."

And on that note, even if gold isn't the absolute *perfect* choice for our monetary system, it surely beats the blatant fraud and exploitation inherent in the system we have today.

So far we've seen how trade first began as barter, and *from* barter came the discovery that certain commodities were always in demand. Those commodities, (sheep, wheat, corn, etc.) became the first form of *commodity money*; widely accepted as payment for other products and services. Commodity money evolved, eventually leading to the use of metal coins and then finally to the use of gold (and silver) as the most widely sought and accepted coins.

But these coins also had their limitations. First, they were heavy. Today, we take for granted that we can carry $1,000 in paper money as easily as we can carry $1. This wasn't the case in a silver or gold coin economy...$1,000 worth of coins weighed 1,000 times more than $1 worth. Also, if you accumulated a significant amount of money, you had to seriously worry about how to keep that money "safe." (Lugging a large quantity of gold and silver around with you wasn't practical and trying to find a truly secure hiding place wasn't so great either.) *Receipt money* emerged as the solution to these problems. Receipt money, as it first began, is an example of a **legitimate** form of paper money. Here is how it came into being.

Receipt Money is born

Goldsmiths handled large stockpiles of gold and silver in their trade. Logically they needed a safe place to store those stockpiles and, for this purpose, they built very strong and well-guarded vaults. Citizens eventually figured out there was no need to worry about hiding their own coins because, for a small fee, they could simply store them in the goldsmith's vault. The goldsmiths happily agreed to the arrangement as it was a way to earn some easy extra money.

As a citizen renting space in the goldsmith's vault, you would take in your supply of gold coins (say $1,000 worth) and you would be given a *receipt* as proof of your deposit. The receipt would state the value of the gold coins you'd deposited (in this case $1,000) and it would be stamped *payable on demand*. This meant, whenever you decided to present the receipt to the goldsmith, he was required to take it from you and, in exchange, give you back your gold. However, it was rare for people to withdraw their gold. (They would just need to find another place to store it if they did.) Instead, most just continued making deposits and collecting receipts as proof of each deposit they'd made.

Soon enough everyone was walking around with these paper receipts in their pockets. Because the paper receipts literally were "good as gold," people began using the receipts to purchase products and services. As an example, if you wanted to purchase an item for $1,000, rather than go to the goldsmith to withdraw your gold coins you'd simply give the seller your $1,000 receipt. This not only made it easier on you, it was easier on the seller too. (If you had paid in gold coins, chances are the seller would have just taken the coins right back to the goldsmith for safe storage.)

This paper "receipt money" (100% backed by gold) was a huge improvement in the evolution of money. It was improved even further when different denominations of receipts were made available at the time of deposit. For instance, if you brought $1,000 worth of coins to the goldsmith, you could now ask for (10) $100 receipts or (20) $50 receipts (etc.) instead of just a single $1,000 receipt. This of course led to the receipts themselves being exchanged for different denominations. (If you had a $100 receipt, you could easily exchange it for (10) $10 receipts, so on and so forth.) It was *honest money* at its best. ...But it didn't last long.

Fractional Money is born

Receipt money made trading with others easier than ever. It was light, easily divisible, didn't need food or water, never "went bad," and was backed 100% by a commodity preferred by all. As a result of its use, communities flourished and individuals prospered. But just as so many before them, the goldsmiths could not resist their temptation to corrupt the money supply in pursuit of illegitimate profits.

As noted, it was very rare for individuals to "cash in" their receipts and withdraw actual coins. The goldsmiths realized at any given time, 90% or more of all coin deposits were left untouched. This sparked an idea. Why leave all that gold gathering dust in the vault when instead it could be loaned out (at interest) to earn a profit? Where once the goldsmith was limited to loaning out what belonged to him (a tiny amount of what was held in the vault) he now could earn ten times as much, or more, loaning out what belonged to others. It would be a profitable little secret known only to him and others in his trade.

This of course was pure fraud. Every coin in the vault had an equivalent "receipt" which was held by the coin's rightful owner. Those who had accepted these receipts in exchange for their coin deposits and those in the community who accepted these receipts as payment for their products and services believed them to be no different than receiving the actual coins themselves. Instead, unbeknownst to the receipt holders, the receipts they held were now only backed by a *fraction* of the value stamped on their face. What began as "receipt money" had now evolved into a new form; it was now *fractional* money.

To easily understand the problem, imagine I ask you to sell me a one-ounce gold coin. To purchase the coin, I pay you with receipt money *equal in value* to the coin itself. (The receipt represents one ounce of gold sitting safely in the goldsmith's vault – *or so you think.*) In reality, what I've given you is a receipt that is only *partially* backed by gold... no different than if I traded you half of a coin for a whole coin. Would you *knowingly* agree to such a "deal?" Would you ever trade half a coin for a whole coin? Of course not.

But you *would* agree to the deal if you didn't know any better, and that was the problem. Nobody knew the coins (supposedly backing each receipt 100%) were being *loaned* to others. And when the people finally *did* discover their coins were being loaned (without their permission), they still didn't comprehend the seriousness of the problem. Sure, they were outraged, but not because they understood the dangers or inherent fraud of fractional money; no, they were upset because the goldsmiths were getting rich loaning out *their coins*!

Well, making tons of money had never been so easy for the goldsmiths; the last thing they wanted was to see it end. So, to calm their depositors (and continue earning big bucks loaning coins that didn't belong to them), they made the following offer: Depositors could now store all their coins in the vault *free of charge* AND (as if that generous offer weren't enough) depositors would also be paid a percentage of the value of the coins they kept in storage! (Let's say 5 %.)

This was a *very clever* solution. Not only would tons of gold start flowing into the goldsmith's vault, it was even less likely that depositors would ever withdraw any of their coins because to do so would only reduce their own earnings.

The average citizen's view was a little less sophisticated than that of the goldsmith. They were certain they'd hammered out a great deal. (1) They'd get to continue using their convenient paper/receipt money, (2) they'd no longer have to pay a storage fee for their coins AND (3) they'd earn some extra money on the side. The goldsmith, all of a sudden, "wasn't such a bad guy after all..."

While it's true the people had solved the problem of "the goldsmith earning all the money" on *their* coin deposits, two bigger problems (the inflation of the money supply and the threat that posed to their wealth) had not been solved. Nor were either of these two problems understood by the general public. Let's briefly cover them both.

Inflation

Assume a depositor places $1,000 worth of gold coins in the goldsmith's vault and, in exchange, receives $1,000 worth of receipts. The community's money supply will not change as a result of this transaction. (Where there once was $1,000 in gold coins circulating in the economy, there is now $1,000 in receipts. And if the receipt holder returns to withdraw his coins, he must surrender his $1,000 worth of receipts to the goldsmith. Any way you slice it, there will be either $1,000 in gold coins circulating or $1,000 in receipts, not both.)

However, under the "fractional money" system something different happens. Our depositor still comes in with $1,000 in gold coins, and he still receives $1,000 in receipts. No problem there. But an hour later, another man comes in. He doesn't want to make a deposit; he wants to *borrow* $1,000. The goldsmith agrees to the loan and issues the borrower $1,000 worth of NEW receipts. In our first example the money supply did not change, but in this example the money supply has doubled. (There is now $2,000 worth of receipts circulating in the economy backed by only $1,000 in gold coins.)

Threat to Depositor's Wealth

Aside from the inflation, there is also another big problem. Say the borrower takes his "newly printed" $1,000 worth of receipts and spends them at a local store. And say the store owner decides he'd rather have the actual gold coins instead of the paper. No problem there. The store owner can take the receipts to the goldsmith, cash them in for coins and be on his way.

But what happens if an hour later the man who made the original deposit shows up to withdraw his coins? Let's say he decided he'd rather just store his gold himself. Too bad for him, his gold walked out the door an hour earlier. This is a highly simplified example, but it illustrates what happens when a banker/goldsmith makes more promises to "pay on demand" than he can honor. The banker/goldsmith cannot produce the coins, he is bankrupt, and he takes the depositor down with him.

Now in the simplified example above, the goldsmith got into trouble by pushing his reserves down to 50%. (The goldsmith held $1,000 in coins to "back" the $2,000 in receipts he issued. That puts the *fraction* of *reserves* at 50 %.) However, it's very unlikely he'd ever get into trouble at that level.

In reality, there are hundreds or thousands of depositors and the vast majority of them are happy to leave their coins in the vault earning interest. Additionally, those who receive the receipts in commerce aren't likely to come in and request coins either because the paper receipts are much more convenient to carry and use. The goldsmith knows this. He's seen first hand that customer demand for actual *coins* is very low. So what inevitably happens is, the goldsmith/banker continues to push down the reserves more and more, always walking closer to the edge of insolvency. Why? Because every time he "creates more receipts" and loans them out, he earns more interest.

Returning to our simplified example, consider the following: A man deposits $1,000 in coins with the goldsmith and receives $1,000 in receipts. In addition, the goldsmith has agreed to pay the man a percentage of the value of his deposit. We'll assume that percentage is 5% per year. To earn the money to pay this 5%, the goldsmith prints up an extra $1,000 in receipts and loans them out at say 8% interest. That leaves the goldsmith a profit of 3% on money he "created out of nothing." (The goldsmith earns 8% on the newly created receipts; he pays the original depositor 5%, and that leaves a 3% profit.)

But in this example, the goldsmith has only doubled the money supply. He still has 50% reserves and that is far more than he needs, so the game continues. What if he quadruples the money supply? Instead of earning just 3% per year on the original $1,000 deposit, the goldsmith's profits soar to 19%! That is over 6 times as much profit as he earned originally, and he is still only down to a 25% reserve ratio.

Here is the math: Instead of creating a single $1,000 loan, this time the goldsmith creates a total of **three** $1,000 loans. Add the original $1,000 worth of receipts (issued to the depositor) to the $3,000 worth of receipts *loaned* to borrowers, and you get $4,000 in total receipts *backed by* only $1,000 worth of coins. (That puts the reserve ratio at 25%.) As in our first example, the first $1,000 loan only produces a profit of 3% for the goldsmith (8% minus 5% paid to the depositor.) However, EACH of the next two loans generates a full 8% for the goldsmith. So, 3% profit on the first loan, plus 16% total on the next two loans means the goldsmith earns 19% on money he created out of nothing.

But the goldsmith still has far more reserves than he feels he needs. From what he can tell, he thinks he can push his reserves down to 10% and still be OK. So he decides to expand the money supply some more, A LOT MORE. If he multiplies the money supply by 8 times, he still will have reserves of 12.5%, and his profits will soar to 51%![17] Sure, the money supply is being diluted, inflation is wreaking its havoc, and the depositors are blissfully unaware how close they are to losing everything, but the goldsmith is literally making money by simply "creating it" out of thin air! Who would want to interrupt something as marvelous as that?

If the goldsmith charges more for his loans, things get even more exciting. Even a small increase in the loan rate increases profits significantly. For instance, with his reserves at 12.5% and loaning at 8%, he earns more than a 50% annual profit on every $1,000 of his depositor's money. But if he loans at an interest rate of 10%, he earns more than 60%! And at 15%, he earns nearly 100%!! At that rate, for every $1 million he attracts in deposits, he can earn nearly $1 million for himself!

---

17   The math: The original depositor is issued $1,000 in receipts for his gold. $7000 in **additional** receipts are created for the purpose of lending. The first loan of $1,000 generates only 3% profit, but the remaining 6 loans earn a full 8% each! This adds up to a total profit, on money created out of nothing, of 51%! (3% on the first loan + 48% total on the other six.)

But wait; maybe he can inflate the money supply even more. Maybe he can get by with driving reserves down to only 6.25%, more than DOUBLING his profits yet again. …Maybe 3%, maybe even 1%!!! The game is intoxicating and it always leads to disaster for depositors. Inevitably, the scam collapses when people realize the receipts they're holding are only worth a small fraction of what is printed on them. A one-ounce gold receipt might only be backed by a tenth of an ounce of gold (or less). When the truth is discovered, a "run on the bank" ensues and only the first few in line are able to withdraw gold. All the rest, the vast majority, are left holding worthless paper.

One would think, after witnessing the aforementioned disaster unfold repeatedly, that bankers would realize the error of their inflationary ways. One would think they'd devise an *honest* monetary system; a system that permits them to earn legitimate profits without exploiting (if not completely ruining) the people who depend on it. One would think… Instead, they set out to devise a sort of "banker's utopia" where they could expand their fraud, operate with ZERO reserves of gold and silver, and shift any losses they might incur on to others. And that brings us to the final form of money we'll be discussing in this chapter: Fiat money.

Once the idea of *fractional* money is accepted, the *fraction* is inevitably pushed down to zero, at which point the money becomes nothing more than pure fiat. Fiat money is money backed by absolutely nothing. It's the equivalent of the "wooden coins" mentioned earlier; inherently worthless. And because fiat money is inherently worthless, the people must be *forced* to accept it via legal tender laws.

Fiat Money

"The *American Heritage Dictionary* defines fiat money as "paper money decreed legal tender, not backed by gold or silver." The two characteristics of fiat money, therefore, are (1) it does not represent anything of intrinsic value and (2) it is decreed legal tender. Legal tender simply means that there is a law requiring everyone to accept the currency in commerce. ...when governments issue fiat money, they always declare it to be legal tender under pain of fine or imprisonment. The only way a government can exchange its worthless paper money for tangible goods and services is to give its citizens no choice.

...The first recorded appearance of fiat money was in thirteenth century China, but its use on a major scale did not occur until colonial America. The experience was disastrous, leading to massive inflation, unemployment, loss of property, and political unrest."

The first paragraph above provides a perfect definition of fiat money, so let's expand on the second paragraph; the track record of fiat money in colonial America.

Fiat money first appeared in Massachusetts following a failed military campaign against Quebec in 1690. Previous expeditions had been successful, but this time Massachusetts had seized nothing of value and, as such, could not pay her troops. Raising taxes would have been very unpopular; a risky proposition. However, ignoring the obligation to pay her troops what they'd been promised was even riskier. Desperate to discharge her debt, the government of

Massachusetts decided to simply print the money. Other colonies watched in amazement and before long, they too were enjoying the *magic* of printing their own cash (and the citizens *enjoyed* the consequences).

As the printing presses inflated the money supply, legal tender laws were instituted to ensure the worthless paper was accepted. Predictably, gold and silver coins disappeared from circulation in the colonies. (Why pay with real money when all you could expect was fiat paper in return?) The only time gold and silver coins *were* spent was with foreigners who demanded *real money* as payment for their products and services. This steadily drained the colonies' total supply of gold and silver. As the supply of gold and silver dwindled, international trade nearly ceased. (Foreigners had no interest in trading their products for fiat paper; who could blame them?)

As the inevitable problems of an inflationary "fiat money system" began to surface, the colonial governments took steps to *fix* the problems. In 1703, South Carolina threatened citizens who refused its paper with fines "*double the value of the bills so refused.*" That didn't work, so in 1716 it increased fines to "*treble the value.*" Some colonies began printing new money to soak up some of the old. For instance, in 1737 Massachusetts traded its citizens $1 of *new* fiat money for $3 worth of their old money, with the added promise the new money would be fully redeemable in gold or silver in five years. (A promise that wasn't kept.)

"By the late 1750s, Connecticut had prices inflated by 800%. The Carolinas had inflated 900%.

Massachusetts 1000%. Rhode Island 2300%. Naturally, these inflations all had to come to an end and, when they did, they turned into equally massive deflations and depressions. It has been shown that, even in colonial times, the classic booms and busts which modern economists are fond of blaming on an "unbridled free market" actually were direct manifestations of the expansion and contraction of fiat money which no longer was governed by the laws of supply and demand."

This downward spiral was temporarily brought to a halt by, of all things, British intervention. The Bank of England, using its influence with the Crown, sought to force the American Colonies to use *its* paper money. The Bank got its way in 1751 when the British Parliament began putting heavy pressure on the colonies to withdraw their currency from circulation. The pressure was increased until, in 1764, the British Parliament passed the "Currency Act" which made it illegal for the colonies to issue paper currency in any form.

Despite major opposition, the Currency Act actually ended up working to the benefit of the colonies. Rather than accept Bank of England money as a primary medium of exchange, the colonists simply returned to a true commodity-based monetary system. The remaining gold and silver coins began to circulate again and other commodities, like tobacco, also served as money. Returning to an honest money system produced immediate results.

"Trade and production rose dramatically and this in turn attracted an inflow of gold and silver coin from around the world, filling the void that had been created by years of worthless paper. ...After the colonies had returned to coin, prices quickly found their natural equilibrium and then stayed at that point..."

Unfortunately, the recovery was short-lived.

The Colonies Declare Their Independence – Fiat Money Returns

Wars are very expensive and it's rare for them to be fought using existing government funds. The American War for Independence was no exception. Faced with a shortage of money, the leaders of the revolution had the usual options available to finance the war:

- They could look to borrow the funds, but that would put them at the mercy of their lenders. Even if the colonies were heavily favored to win their battle against Great Britain, there would be limits to how much lenders could produce or would be willing to risk. And, up against the most dominant military in the world, the colonies were anything but "heavily favored to win."

- They could try to raise the money via taxation but (as is often the case) taxes sufficient to fully fund the war would have been severe. Support for this approach would have been very difficult to sustain.

- Finally, there was the path of least resistance, the printing press. Arguably, this approach ends up *costing* the most, but as G. Edward Griffin explains:

> "By artificially increasing the money supply…
> the real cost is hidden from view. It is still paid,
> of course, but through inflation, a process that
> few people understand."

Between 1775 and 1779, the central government expanded the total money supply from just $12 million to a whopping $425 million. That's an increase of more than 3,500%. In addition, the individual states were busy doing the same thing. It's been estimated, in just five years, the total expansion reached 5,000%.

> "The first exhilarating effect of this flood of new
> money was the flush of apparent prosperity, but
> that was quickly followed by inflation as the self-
> destruct mechanism began to operate. In 1775, paper
> Continentals were traded for one dollar in gold. In
> 1777, they were exchanged for twenty-five cents.
> By 1779, just four years from their issue, they were
> worth less than a penny…it was in that year George
> Washington wrote, '*A wagon load of money will
> scarcely purchase a wagon load of provisions.*'"

Fiat money might provide instant purchasing power for those who create it, but it does so at the expense of those who are forced to use it. Every dollar worth of products and services it buys is extracted from the citizens via the hidden tax of inflation. As stated in chapter one, it makes little difference whether the government takes $3,000 worth of your purchasing power by direct taxation, or takes $3,000 of your purchasing power through an inflationary policy; the effect on your wealth is the same. You're $3,000 *weaker* in either case.

That said, there *are* many aspects that make inflation a far more insidious tax:

- Those on fixed incomes or who have actually saved their money are hit the hardest.

- Whereas normal taxation *cannot* be hidden from the people (placing firm limits on its use), inflation allows purchasing power to be confiscated *secretly*. Like theft, there isn't even the illusion of an agreement between those who are taking the money and those who are surrendering it. Purchasing power taken from citizens in this fashion is *abusive* in and of itself. That so few understand the process only makes it easier for the *abusers*.

- So long as the citizens are forced to use the fiat currency, there is nothing they can do to stop the confiscation of their money. $10,000 under the mattress today might only be worth $5,000 in actual purchasing power next month. (Consider the case of the Continentals. At the end of four years, what began as $10,000 worth of purchasing power deteriorated to only $100! That's no different than looking under your mattress to find somebody took $9,900 of what you had saved.)

The massive inflation caused economic chaos and that was soon followed by attempts to *fix* the problems. (Sound familiar?) As prices went through the roof ($5,000 for a pair of shoes, $1 million for a suite of clothes, etc.), the colonies instituted wage and price controls. When that wasn't enough, severe legal tender laws were enacted to further *encourage* people to be good patriots. According to this law, refusing the worthless currency was tantamount to treason:

> "If any person shall hereafter be so lost to all virtue and regard for his Country as to refuse to receive said bills in payment...he shall be deemed, published, and treated as an enemy in this Country and precluded from all trade or intercourse with the inhabitants of these colonies."

And as night follows day, the chaos of inflation was followed by the chaos of deflation. As the bubble burst, unemployment, bankruptcies, foreclosures, even riots and insurrection, appeared in its wake. The full *costs* would finally be counted.

> "Prices fell drastically, which was wonderful for those who were buying. But, for the merchants who were *selling* or the farmers who had borrowed heavily to acquire property at inflated wartime prices, it was a disaster.
>
> The new, lower prices were not adequate to sustain their fixed, inflated mortgages, and many hard-working families were ruined...Idleness and economic depression also led to outbursts of rebellion and insurrection. George Washington wrote: *'If...any person had told me that there would have been such formidable rebellion as exists, I would have thought him...a fit subject for a madhouse.'*"

When our founding fathers drafted our Constitution, the pain and suffering of fiat money was still fresh in their minds. They firmly resolved to rid our nation of it once and for all.

As a result, the United States of America became the most powerful economic force the world had ever seen.

But the wisdom of our nation's founders was lost with the passage of time, allowing those who benefit from "fractional reserve" and/or purely "fiat money" systems to steal their way back into power. In the next chapter, we'll delve deeper into the *"unbroken record of fraud, booms, busts, and economic chaos"*[18] of their *dishonest* money.

---

18 Griffin

CHAPTER 7
The World's First Central Bank

"It is significant that the Bank of England was launched to help the English government finance a large deficit. Governments everywhere and at all times are short of money...The reason is simple: unlike private persons or firms, who obtain money by selling needed goods and services to others... Governments can only obtain money by grabbing it from others, and therefore they are always on the lookout to find new and ingenious ways of doing the grabbing. Taxation is the standard method; but, at least until the twentieth century, the people were very edgy about taxes, and any increase in a tax or imposition of a new tax was likely to land the government in revolutionary hot water." –Murray Rothbard, *The Case Against the Fed*

England in a bind

Financially drained by 50 years of war against France (as well as numerous civil wars fought largely over excessive taxation), England was in desperate need of new revenue.

Specifically, King William was not only broke in 1693, he was in the middle of the "War of the Grand Alliance" and his options for obtaining money were very thin.

He could try to raise taxes, but then again he could also wind up with another civil war on his hands. He could try to borrow the money, but just 20 years earlier his predecessor (King Charles II) flatly refused to repay over a million pounds he'd borrowed. This betrayal wiped out the savings of thousands of individuals and, logically enough, did nothing to boost enthusiasm for "lending money to The Crown."

King William could try printing his own fiat currency, but even that seemed unlikely to work. You see, King Charles II had done that too and the currency was never widely accepted. (Given a choice between real money and fiat money, issued under the "authority of The Crown" but backed by absolutely nothing, the people always preferred the real thing.) If only there was a way to print fiat money and have people accept it as real money...if only there was a way. Perhaps, with a little creativity, there was.

Let's back up for just a minute. Pretend King William's credit was fantastic. Pretend he had no problem borrowing the *real money* he needed to finance his war. We'll say a group of bankers contacted him at the height of his financial problems and said: *"King William, we'll happily buy every war bond you want to sell. We know you'll make your interest payments on time and, when it's time for us to cash in our bonds, you'll pay us in full on demand...we trust you 100%."*

If this scenario were true, the King could easily raise all the money he needed. It would come directly from the bankers in the form of gold (or receipts fully backed by gold) and the King could then easily pay his soldiers, suppliers, etc. without worrying about his payments being rejected. The bankers would make a fortune financing the war and the King would have his money. Everyone (except those fighting and dying of course) would win...and what could be better than that?

So the bankers, being the unscrupulous but highly intelligent lot they were, came up with an *ingenious* plan. If the King would grant them an exclusive license (a monopoly) to issue England's paper currency, the bankers (in return) would loan the King all the money he needed. The money for his loans would be created out of nothing (backed by only a fraction of coin) but nobody would know that.

> "The newly created bills and notes were indistinguishable from those previously backed by coin, and the public was none the wiser." (This guaranteed the currency would be) "...accepted at full face value in payment for the expenses of war."

> "In this first official act of the world's first central bank can be seen the grand pretense that has characterized all those which have followed. The Bank" (of England) "pretended to make a loan but what it really did was to manufacture the money for government's use. If the government had done this directly, the fiat nature of the currency would have been immediately recognized, and it probably would not have been accepted at full face value..."

But the Bank of England also received other privileges for agreeing to *assist* the government. Not only did the bank get to create money out of nothing and loan it to the government at 8% interest, it was also permitted to count the government bonds as *reserves,* giving it the ability to create even more money out of nothing for loans to the general public.

So basically, it goes like this: The government has no money so it creates a bond. (The bond is nothing more than a piece of paper with a dollar amount printed on it, or in this case a *Pound* "£" amount, printed on it.) The government then offers the bond as collateral for a loan. Rather than purchase the bond with real money, the Bank of England simply "creates money out of thin air" in the amount needed. The bank can now collect 8% interest on the *money* it just loaned to the government. (If the bond is valued at £1,000,000, the bank will earn £80,000 per year in interest/profit.)

But wait, there's more! The Bank is also permitted to count the bond's printed value the same as it would an equal amount of gold. In other words, using the bond as "reserves," it can now print another pile of money (equal to whatever is printed on the bond) and loan *that* out at interest too! Must be nice, huh?

Rothbard writes:

> "In short, since there were not enough private savers willing to finance the deficit, Paterson and his group" (the men behind the Bank of England) "were graciously willing to buy government bonds, provided they could do so with newly-created out-of-thin-air bank notes carrying a raft of special

privileges with them. This was a splendid deal for Paterson and company, and the government benefited from the flimflam of a seemingly legitimate bank's financing... As soon as the Bank of England was chartered in 1694, King William himself and various members of Parliament rushed to become shareholders of the new money factory they had just created."

As if the millions in newly created "Bank of England" notes weren't bad enough for the economy, banks outside of London were permitted to use gold *OR* Bank of England notes as reserves for the money they issued. So, assuming the permissible "fraction" of reserves was 50%, that meant these country banks could create two new units of *their* currency for every single Bank of England note they held in their vaults. All of this new money flooded the economy and within just two years, prices had more than doubled. Predictably, people began to lose faith in the currency. That was followed by a run on the Bank and, "surprise, surprise," the Bank of England did not have enough gold coin to satisfy the demand.

With that, the fraudulent nature of the new currency was exposed and the scam was over...or was it? King William still needed the Bank, and the Bank needed King William. In short, like any cabal, the conspirators needed each other to protect their own interests.

"When banks cannot honor their contracts to deliver coin in return for their receipts, they are, in fact, bankrupt. They should be allowed to go out of business and liquidate their assets to satisfy their creditors. ...That, of course, was not allowed to happen. The Cabal is a *partnership*, and each of the two groups is committed to protect each other, not out of loyalty, but out of mutual self interest. ...In May of 1696, just two years after the Bank was formed, a law was passed authorizing it to suspend payment in specie." (Gold) "By force of law, the Bank was now exempted from having to honor its contract to return the gold.

This was a fateful event in the history of money, because the precedent has been followed ever since. In Europe and America, the banks have always operated with the assumption that their partners in government will come to their aid when they get into trouble. Politicians may speak about "protecting the public," but the underlying reality is that the government *needs* the fiat money produced by the banks. The banks, therefore – at least the big ones – must not be allowed to fail. Only a cartel with government protection can enjoy such insulation from the workings of a free market."

No longer obligated to redeem their paper in gold, the banks went to work creating ever larger quantities of money. The result was more inflation and more suffering for the general public. But not for the cabal; King William benefited from the mechanism of extracting purchasing power from the people via inflation, and the bankers reaped the rewards of loaning massive amounts of money created out of nothing. And the game continued.

Fast forward about 100 years: Concerned about rising gold prices, the British Government assembled a special committee in 1810 to determine the cause of (and a solution to) the problem. The final report hit the nail on the head: Gold prices weren't rising; the purchasing power of the currency was going down. Too much money was being created and dumped into the economy. Piles of new money (chasing the same amount of products and services) were driving prices up. More importantly, the committee correctly identified the solution: Bank of England notes should be made fully convertible into gold coin. This would limit the amount of paper currency that could be created to the amount of gold held in bank vaults and prices would stabilize.

Although everyone agreed with the solution, the war with Napoleon ensured it wouldn't be implemented. England needed to extract purchasing power from its citizens to pay for the war, and the bankers provided a sneaky way to do so. (Just something to consider: A wise businessman determines where his biggest profits come from and *focuses* on that market. How long do you suppose it took the bankers to figure out that "governments at war" were their best customers? At some point they must have realized that "war" guaranteed their mechanism for generating enormous profits, on money created out of nothing, would be safe.)

Prices continued to rise and by 1815 they had again doubled. This was followed by a strong downward correction, plunging England into a deep depression. The monetary system was an inexcusable mess and so, after the war with Napoleon ended, the Bank of England was required to again redeem its notes in gold. But it was not a *true* 100% gold standard; it was merely a fractional reserve system. The Bank still created money out of nothing for the purpose of lending and within

4 years of implementing the new "safe fractional limits," a brief inflationary *boom* was followed by an inevitable *bust*. Countless fortunes were wiped out and England was again thrust into depression.

By 1839, demands for a legitimate solution to England's booms and busts had grown too loud to ignore. After 5 years of intense analysis and debate, the Peel Act was passed in 1844. Unfortunately, the act was a political compromise and fell far short of what was required to correct the problem. Even its attempts to limit the amount of paper currency banks could create proved largely irrelevant. That's because the act did nothing to limit the amount of "checkbook money" a bank could create. In other words, the bank might have been prevented from creating £1 million in paper currency for a loan, but there was nothing to stop it from simply typing a £1 million balance into a borrower's checking account.

> "Within three years of the "reform," England faced another crisis with still more bank failures and more losses to depositors. But when the Bank of England tottered on the edge of insolvency, once again the government intervened. In 1847 the Bank was exempted from the legal reserve requirements of the Peel Act. Such is the rock-steady dependability of man-made limits to the money supply.
>
> It is an incredible fact of history that, in spite of the…recurring failures…during these years, the central-bank mechanism was so attractive to the political and monetary scientists that it became the model for all of Europe. The Bank of Prussia became the Reichsbank. Napoleon established

the Banque de France. A few decades later, the concept became the venerated model for the Federal Reserve System. Who cares if the scheme is destructive? Here is the perfect tool for obtaining unlimited funding for politicians and endless profits for bankers. And best of all, **the little people who pay the bills for both groups have practically no idea what is being done to them.**" (Emphasis added.)

Believe it or not, history actually does provide us a few examples of *honest* banking. The Banca della Piazza del Rialto is one such case. Sustaining itself solely on service fees (from storing coins, exchanging currencies, notary services, and facilitating payments between customers), the bank not only prospered, it became the center of Venetian commerce. In fact, the bank became so trusted, its paper currency actually traded at a *premium* over coins!

To understand how this is possible, consider an economy with many different kinds of coins being traded; some of them shaved, some heavily worn, some debased with other metals. It wasn't easy for an average citizen to perfectly determine each coin's worth. But this was precisely the kind of expertise the bank brought to the table. Depositors brought their coins to the bank; the bank carefully examined the coins to determine their value and then issued a proper amount of receipts.

"The public, therefore, was far more certain of the value of the" (bank's) "paper receipts than of many of the coins and, consequently, was willing to exchange a little bit more for them."

Unfortunately, politicians eventually succumbed to the temptation of creating money out of nothing and that was the end of that.

The Bank of Amsterdam provides another example. By limiting itself to honest banking, the Bank's paper currency became the preferred method of making and receiving payments in and around Amsterdam. Its paper also carried a premium. However, once this level of trust had been established, the temptation to exploit it was (apparently) too great to resist. The Bank began creating additional currency (money out of nothing) and although it enjoyed the immediate profits, it also reaped the inevitable harvest... insolvency.

Germany's Bank of Hamburg provides our final example.

> "For over two centuries it faithfully adhered to the principle of safe deposit. So scrupulous was its administration that, when Napoleon took possession of the bank in 1813, he found 7,506,956 marks in silver held against liabilities of 7,489,343. That was 17,613 *more* than was actually needed. ...Because of foreign invasion, the bank's currency was no longer fully convertible into coin as receipt money. It was now *fractional* money, and the self-destruct mechanism had been set in motion. The bank lasted another fifty-five years until 1871 when it was ordered to liquidate all of its accounts. ...That is the end of the short story of honest banking. From that point forward, fractional-reserve banking became the universal practice."

The fraudulent "fractional reserve" system continues to this day. However, unlike its earlier incarnations, the game is now more sophisticated (and far more profitable). At least the pioneers of the scam kept *some* gold or silver as *reserves* to back their *loans* of *new money* (created out of nothing). Today, the "reserves" that banks rely on to create new money have no intrinsic value whatsoever. In other words, where once a bank might issue paper money equal to ten times the value of the gold or silver coins they held in their vault, today there isn't a single ounce of gold or silver backing our currency. Today, our money is created using nothing but fiat **paper and computer entries** as *reserves*! There is no *real* money anywhere. Even worse (yes, there is a "worse"), every dollar in circulation is inextricably tied to debt. What we're forced to use today **is WORSE than** fiat money, **it is _debt money._**

That last sentence is the real kicker. Our entire monetary system, as it now stands, is based on nothing but debt. Every physical dollar, as well as every digital dollar, had to be *borrowed* into existence. So long as our entire money supply is made up of this *debt money*, the bankers are guaranteed to earn interest on every single dollar, every moment it exists. It also means our debt is inescapable. To pay off every loan, we'd have to give back every dollar the bankers have created. This would reduce our money supply to zero...it can't be done.

> "Robert Hemphill was the Credit Manager of the Federal Reserve Bank in Atlanta. In the foreword to a book by Irving Fisher, entitled *100% Money*, Hemphill said this:

'If all the bank loans were paid, no one could have a bank deposit, and there would not be a dollar of coin or currency in circulation. This is a staggering thought. We are completely dependent on the commercial banks. Someone has to borrow every dollar we have in circulation, cash, or credit. If the banks create ample synthetic money we are prosperous; if not, we starve. We are absolutely without a permanent money system. When one gets a complete grasp of the picture, the tragic absurdity of our hopeless situation is almost incredible—but there it is.' "

So the bankers not only profit from this *debt money* system, they've structured their business in such a way that we (operating within the rules of the system) can never escape it. Who in their right mind would hand over this kind of power and control to an unelected group of financial elites? It's nothing short of economic slavery.

It's important to remember, we're in this mess not just because of the "unscrupulous but highly intelligent" individuals who conspired to gain control of our nation's money supply, but also because of our elected officials who handed it over and continue to support (and benefit from) the arrangement.

CHAPTER 8
How They Do It

Ok, now it is time to show exactly *how* the Federal Reserve System creates money out of nothing. But before we do that, let's quickly recap the different forms of money discussed up to this point.

1. *Commodity money:*
Commodity money is any form of money that has intrinsic value. Sheep, cows, corn, wheat; all of these served as early forms of commodity money. When mankind discovered metal and learned to craft it into tools and weapons, the metals themselves became a new (more convenient) form of commodity money. Unlike livestock, metal didn't need to be fed, watered and cleaned up after. And, unlike wheat and corn, you didn't have to worry about metal *going bad*, becoming contaminated with bugs or mold, etc.

Also, metal was easily divisible. Assuming a cow was equal in value to 100 pounds of iron, and an item was for sale valued at 10 pounds of iron (or "1/10th" of a cow), the individual buying with iron had a distinct advantage; he could easily produce the exact amount of money needed. For these reasons, metal became the most common form of commodity money. Though different metals were used (iron, tin, copper, etc.), gold and silver coins became the standard.

2. *Receipt money*:

Gold and silver coins were a much improved form of commodity money, but they still had some drawbacks. For instance, if you were even moderately wealthy, carrying all of your gold or silver coins around with you was cumbersome and potentially dangerous. Finding a place to safely hide your coins wasn't easy either.

Seeing an opportunity to earn a little extra money, goldsmiths solved this problem by renting storage space in their vaults. When a citizen came in to deposit their coins, the goldsmith would give them a paper receipt as proof of their deposit. So, if a customer deposited $1,000 in gold coins, they were given a receipt (or receipts) valued at $1,000 worth of gold.

These receipts were "payable on demand" meaning the depositor, at any time, could come in and exchange the receipts for their gold. Because they were literally "good as gold," citizens began accepting the receipts as payment for products and services. From that point forward the receipts became a legitimate form of paper money, 100% *backed by* gold (or sometimes backed by silver).

As time passed, it became increasingly rare for individuals to visit the goldsmith and demand coins in exchange for their receipts. (Although receipt holders had the right to exchange their receipts for gold at any time, they were happy to leave it locked up in the goldsmith's vault.) It was much more convenient to use the paper money, instead of the physical coins they represented, in commerce.

3. *Fractional Money*:

At some point, the goldsmiths realized that almost nobody ever came in to withdraw their coins, and this sparked an idea. Why leave all that gold gathering dust in the vault (earning only a small storage fee) when instead it could be loaned out (at interest) for a much greater profit? Since receipt money was already in use, the goldsmith wouldn't even have to remove the coins from storage. When a borrower came in seeking $1,000, the goldsmith could simply print up $1,000 worth of new receipts!

This, of course, was an act of pure fraud. The goldsmith had no right to give a borrower (or anyone the borrower gave his *borrowed* receipts to) the right to claim somebody else's gold. Additionally, the *only* reason citizens accepted receipts as payment was because they believed the value stamped on every receipt was backed by an equal amount of coins in storage. Unbeknownst to them, this was no longer the case.

What began as legitimate *receipt* money (backed 100% by coins held in reserve) was now *fractional* money. By creating new receipts, the goldsmith had secretly driven down the percentage of "reserves" backing each receipt. (And with each new printing, the fraction became less and less.) Before long, citizens were, unknowingly, accepting receipts backed by only half its printed value, a quarter its printed value, a tenth its printed value. When people finally figured out what was going on, they rushed to exchange their receipts for coin.

Of course, only the first few in line were able to do so. The rest were left holding worthless paper.

4. *Fiat Money:*

Encarta defines fiat money as: *"paper money that a government declares to be legal tender although it is not based on or convertible into coins..."* Another way to put that would be: Fiat money is paper (backed by nothing) and because so, government must *force* people to accept it via legal tender laws.

But believe it or not, there is actually something worse than fiat paper money. And this brings us to the final form of money we'll be discussing in this book. The form of money we're using today is:

5. *Debt Money*:

Take the inherently fraudulent characteristics of a fractional money system; add in the greater fraud of pure fiat, top it off with a mechanism designed to generate inescapable perpetual debt and *presto*: You've got the greatest monetary fraud ever perpetrated against mankind. And, wouldn't you know, you also have all the components that make up our current monetary system. (It is *dishonest money* at its worst.)

Rather than openly print the money it needs to cover its reckless spending, our government uses a less obvious tactic. Make no mistake, it still ends up "creating money out of nothing" for its own purposes, it simply uses its friends at the Federal Reserve to do so. And in exchange for *helping* our government obtain the money it needs, the banking system reaps financial benefits that are nothing short of obscene. (At a cost to our country that is incalculable.)

You see, unlike a normal fiat money system (where the government simply creates its own worthless paper money, spends it into the economy, and demands everyone accept it), our entire money supply is built on **debt**. That means, not a single dollar comes into existence but by the act of *borrowing it* into existence. First let me explain this in the simplest terms possible, and then we'll get into a more detailed explanation.

Assume the government needs (*wants*) 1 billion dollars. Rather than print the money itself, the government goes to its banking buddies at the Federal Reserve. The Federal Reserve is ALWAYS happy to *loan* whatever amount of money the government "needs." The problem is the Fed doesn't actually *loan* anything. Yes, when the government shows up with its 1 billion dollar bond, the Fed will give it a 1 billion dollar check in exchange; but that 1 billion dollar Federal Reserve check doesn't have anything backing it. The *money* (keystrokes in the Fed's computer system) is created on the spot out of thin air; *poof*, there it is.

The government signs its new Federal Reserve check, deposits it in its Federal Reserve bank account, and immediately begins "paying its bills." (Writing checks to government employees, contractors, etc. and inflating our money supply by $1 billion in the process.) But that's just the beginning of the inflation. The government employees, contractors, etc. take their government checks and deposit them in *their* local bank accounts. Now the local banks, using the original

1 billion dollars worth of government checks as *"reserves,"* are permitted to inflate our money supply by another $9 billion! (And they accomplish this by making yet more loans of "money created out of nothing" to businesses, individuals, and government.)

> "The bottom line is that the Congress and the banking cartel have entered into a partnership in which the cartel has the privilege of collecting interest on money which it creates out of nothing, a perpetual override on every American dollar that exists in the world. Congress, on the other hand, has access to unlimited funding without having to tell the voters their taxes are being raised through the process of inflation."

Such is the nature of our entire money supply. Our purchasing power is stolen via inflation, our collective purchasing power is eroded by inescapable interest on every dollar in existence, and if we (as a nation) attempted to pay off any significant portion of our debt, within the rules of the current system, our country would be thrust into economic chaos. Why? Because just as the "debt dollars" are created out of nothing when a loan is issued, they are "erased" when the debt is repaid (and this *deflates* our money supply). But the remaining debt (the only thing keeping ANY *money* in circulation) does not "adjust" downward. As the money supply gets tighter, those who are trapped in high-dollar loans (say home loans based on prices that reflected a larger money supply) will find it increasingly difficult to make their payments. There are simply too few dollars to service the debt *and* fuel the economy. [19]

---

19   For a short and easy article that explains this further, read *Ten Humans and a Banker* in the addendum of this book.

It's sobering to consider, under our current system, there can never be another debt-free generation...not even close. To pay off a large portion of our debt would be disastrous; to pay it all off, impossible. Does this sound like a system designed with *our* best interests in mind?

The Nuts and Bolts

Alright, we've given the easy explanation, now a slightly expanded overview of how the Federal Reserve System creates and expands our nation's *debt money* supply. As in the previous example, we'll focus on the primary method used; it's called the "open market operation."

1. The government needs money, but under our current system it can't just *create it*. So instead, it *creates* the next best thing. The government *"...adds ink to a piece of paper, creates impressive designs around the edges, and calls it a (Treasury) bond or Treasury note." –Griffin.* These pieces of paper are generically referred to as *Treasury Securities* and they are offered as collateral to potential lenders.

As a simple example: The government creates a bond in a denomination of $100,000 with a *maturity date* of ten years. All that means is, a *lender* can acquire the bond for $100,000, he will earn interest on the loan for ten years, and when the bond matures (at the end of ten years) his principal loan amount ($100,000) will be repaid. Treasury securities are offered in many different denominations and *maturity* can vary between 30 days (very short term loan) to 30 years.

SIDE NOTE: If you or I purchase these Treasury securities, it does not *inflate* the nation's money supply. That is because when you or I loan the government money, we are not allowed to create a new pile of money to do it. We must use money we've already earned. The same is true when a business or other institution acquires these securities; money already in circulation must be used. Only Federal Reserve banks, and commercial banks, are allowed to create money out of nothing for the purpose of lending money to the government.

...continuing...

2. The government, looking to convert its "Treasury securities" into something it can spend (Federal Reserve Notes and checkbook money), turns to the Fed. The Fed is happy to oblige. It pulls a check out of its *magic* checkbook, writes in whatever dollar amount is needed, and gives it to the government in exchange for the securities.

"There is no money in any account to cover this check. Anyone else doing this would be sent to prison. It is legal for the Fed, however, because Congress wants the money, and it is the easiest way to get it. (To raise taxes would be political suicide; to depend on the public to buy all the bonds would not be realistic...and to print very large quantities of currency would be obvious and controversial.) This way, the process is mysteriously wrapped up in the banking system. The end result, however, is the same as turning on government printing presses and simply manufacturing fiat money...to pay government expenses."

3. The government endorses its Federal Reserve check, and then deposits it with one of the Federal Reserve banks. The check amount is added to the government's account balance and, just like that, the government can begin spending the money, which it does by writing checks of its own. *"These checks become the means by which the first wave of fiat money floods into the economy. Recipients now deposit them into their own* (commercial) *bank accounts..." –Griffin.* And this is where the ***real* action** begins.

> **SIDE NOTE:** Some like to point out Federal Reserve banks are "not operated for profit" and that they "return to the U.S. Treasury all earnings in excess of Federal Reserve operating expenses." Assuming we accept *all* excess earnings really are handed over (the Fed has never been properly audited; how could we know?), this *fact* is still largely irrelevant. Huge profits are made when *commercial* banks get their hands on the newly created Fed money. (This should come as no surprise; it was the commercial banking interests of Rockefeller, Morgan, Rothschild, Kuhn Loeb, and Warburg that crafted the system.) And if those profits weren't enough, as we've already covered, the biggest *profit* gained in this game is *control.*

...continuing...

4. So assume the government pays Joe Contractor $1 million by check and Joe promptly deposits that check at his commercial bank. Joe is happy because his bank account balance is now 1 million dollars bigger. But the bank is even happier. In accordance with the rules of our Federal Reserve

System, commercial banks only need to keep 10% *reserves* on hand. In short, that means the bank Joe deposited his million dollars with immediately has $900,000 in *"excess reserves."* ($1 million minus 10% in *required reserves* leaves $900,000 *excess reserves*.) Guess what that means? It means the bank is allowed to create $900,000 in *new* money (for loans) out of thin air.

5. But that's not all!!! When that $900,000 in newly created debt money is spent into the economy, it finds its way right back into the banking system as new deposits and those deposits create "excess reserves" too. As a simple example, if the $900,000 all winds up in one bank, that bank is only required to keep 10% of $900,000 *in reserves*. So that means it can now create $810,000 in new loans out of nothing; again the debt money supply increases! And when that newly created $810,000 is deposited, it can be used to create another $729,000 in loans "created out of nothing."

This continues over and over again. By the time the process reaches its *legal* limit, the commercial banks will have created 9 million new debt dollars on top of the original $1 million Federal Reserve *loan* (also created out of thin air) for the government. (A total increase in our money supply of $10 million!) Even if the Fed bank hands over every penny of interest it earns on the $1 million *loan* to the government, the commercial banks can earn ten times as much (or more depending on the interest rates) on the $9 million they created.

Try to imagine the wealth and power you could amass under a system that allowed YOU to do this. Imagine being legally allowed to loan out money that you never had to earn...money that you could simply "create" and then collect interest on. With only 1 billion dollars you could easily generate 50 - 100 million dollars *per year* in interest payments. Even the best among us, given the chance to acquire such a lucrative government-backed monopoly, might find it hard to resist. ...To say nothing of a group of unscrupulous, yet highly intelligent, bankers.

> "The total amount of fiat money created by the Federal Reserve and the commercial banks together is approximately ten times the amount of the underlying government debt. To the degree that this newly created money floods into the economy in excess of goods and services, it causes the purchasing power of all money, both old and new, to decline. Prices go up because the relative value of the money has gone down. The result is the same as if that purchasing power had been taken from us in taxes.

> ...Since our money is an arbitrary entity with nothing behind it except debt, its quantity can go down as well as up. When people are going deeper into debt, the nation's money supply expands and prices go up, when they pay off their debts and refuse to renew, the money supply contracts and prices tumble. This alteration between periods of expansion and contraction of the money supply is the underlying cause of booms, busts, and depressions.

> Who benefits from all of this? Certainly not the average citizen. The only beneficiaries are the political scientists in Congress who enjoy the effect

of unlimited revenue to perpetuate their power, and the monetary scientists within the banking cartel called the Federal Reserve System who have been able to harness the American people, without their knowing it, to the yoke of modern feudalism."

That covers the most common method by which the Fed System inflates our money supply; by "monetizing" government debt. (Converting government IOUs like Treasury bonds into "money" by simply creating the money out of nothing and *loaning* it to the government.) The government spends the money and then commercial banks "inflate" on top of what was originally created. But if the government isn't borrowing enough from the Fed, there are plenty of other ways for "the system" to work its magic.

Another inflation mechanism is known as the "discount window." The discount window is where commercial banks go to borrow money from the Fed. The inflationary process is similar to the open market operation, only a little more direct.

Rather than *loan* the government money (which then becomes government checks, then eventually becomes deposits in commercial banks, then is counted as *reserves*, which then can be multiplied by up to 10 times the original loan amount), the Fed simply *loans* money to the commercial banks directly. It's a much easier process. If a bank borrows $1 million, it can immediately start the process of creating more money. (Subtract 10% for reserves, create $900,000. When the $900,000 makes its way back, subtract 10% for reserves, create $810,000, etc.)

The enormous increase in our nation's money supply leading up to the stock market crash in 1929 (and the Great Depression) was not due to government borrowing. The government, prior to the crash, was doing well and had little need to borrow. No, the bulk of new money originated out of the Fed's discount window. At this point in our history, there is little doubt about whether or not Fed policy *IS* what crashed our economy and led to the Great Depression. It most certainly did. Today, the arguments should be based on whether or not the *monetary scientists*, working through the Fed, did it on purpose. [20]

Another method the Fed *can* use to increase our money supply is to simply change the required "reserve ratios" that commercial banks must hold. The current requirement of 10% is purely arbitrary. If there is a *need* for more money, it could be easily cut in half to 5% (doubling the amount of new money that can be created from deposits), quartered to 2.5%, or even dropped all together. It's the Fed's call.

And as if all this weren't enough, the Monetary Control Act of 1980 handed the Fed even more power. Now, the Fed has the authority to legally *monetize* foreign debt too! (Which it has already done, to the tune of many billions of dollars.)

> "The apparent purpose of this legislation is to…bail out those governments which are having trouble

---

20 Prior to the Great Depression, "gold" was money in the United States. That ended in 1933 when FDR signed executive order 6102, requiring all U.S. citizens to immediately surrender their gold and gold certificates to the Federal Reserve. In exchange for their gold, citizens were given "money" that could NOT be redeemed in gold (because private gold ownership was now illegal). Failure to comply with the order carried a prison sentence of up to 10 years, a $10,000 fine (over $150,000 in today's dollars), or both.

paying the interest on their loans to American banks. When the Fed creates fiat American dollars to give foreign governments in exchange for their worthless bonds, the money path is slightly longer and more twisted, but the effect is similar to the purchase of U.S. Treasury Bonds. ...they flow back into the U.S. money pool (multiplied by nine) in the form of additional loans. The cost of the operation is once again borne by the American citizen through the loss of purchasing power. ...As long as *someone* is willing to borrow American dollars, the cartel will have the option of creating those dollars specifically to purchase their bonds and, by so doing, continue to expand the money supply."

By confiscating and "redistributing" purchasing power, the elite are able to shape the world as they see fit. (Rewarding those who comply with their wishes, and punishing those who insist on *independence*.)

"Income tax" is one way to confiscate purchasing power and, needless to say, it is a real burden on those who actually have to EARN their money. But inflation is a form of taxation too...and because so few understand it, it is the preferred method for shearing the public. Sadly, as the citizens find it harder and harder to get by, they're driven into the arms of the very same people who robbed them.

CHAPTER 9
How We Stop Them

We've been here before

This is not the first or second time "banking elites" have sought to seize control of our monetary system. It is the third.[21] Our first Central Bank, *The Bank of the United States,* was narrowly voted out of existence in 1811. Our second Central Bank, *The 2nd Bank of the United States,* went down kicking and screaming in 1836. Sadly, our third Central Bank, *The Federal Reserve*, was created 77 years later (in 1913) and has been with us ever since. But as our history clearly shows, the Fed only exists because *we* **permit it to**. The hard-fought battle that brought the 2nd Bank of the United States to its knees provides us all the proof we need.

You see, we've already covered the danger of handing over control of our nation's money supply to "unscrupulous, yet highly intelligent bankers." We've covered how the Federal Reserve System has been used (and is *being used)* against us.

---

21 Going back in time to the point where our current "United States Federal Government" was established (as we're doing here), the Fed is only our third Central Bank. If we count the short-lived "Bank of North America" (1781 – 1783) which was established PRIOR to the ratification of our Constitution and Bill of Rights, the Fed would be our *fourth* central bank.

What we haven't covered is what *can* happen when just **ONE** effective leader turns on the financial elite, *bites the hand* that feeds Washington and (with the help of an informed and fed up citizenry) engages the enemy head on. So let's cover that now.

The 2nd Bank of the United States
(Nicholas Biddle vs. Andrew Jackson)

The 2nd Bank of the United States was created in 1816. It was granted a 20-year charter (Federal license) and was headed by Nicholas Biddle. Biddle represented:

> "...the archetype of the new Eastern Establishment: wealthy, arrogant, ruthless, and brilliant. He had graduated from the University of Pennsylvania at the age of only thirteen, and, as a young man entering business, had fully mastered the **secret science of money.** With the ability to control the flow of the nation's credit, Biddle soon became one of the most powerful men in America." (Emphasis added.)

Using the power granted by Congress, Biddle and his merry band of monetary scientists got straight to work. By first heavily inflating the money supply and then suddenly, drastically and deliberately constricting it, they successfully wiped out many of their competitors in the banking industry. (And that translates into a LOT of Americans losing every penny of their savings along with their homes and other possessions.) In fact, the 2nd Bank of the United States had the distinct honor of handing our newly formed republic its first nationwide depression. The ensuing chaos became known as the "Panic of 1819."

> "Starting in July of 1818...the BUS (2nd Bank of the United States) began a series of enormous contractions, forced curtailment of loans, contractions of credit in the south and west...The contractions of money and credit swiftly brought to the United States its first widespread economic and financial depression. ... The result of this contraction was a rash of defaults, bankruptcies of business and manufacturers..."
> –Murray Rothbard

> "The pressure placed upon the state banks deflated the economy drastically, and as the money supply wilted, the country sank into severe depression."
> –Herman Krooss

As the effects of *the Panic of 1819* took hold (hundreds of thousands out of work, unemployment exceeding 70% in some areas, thousands placed in *debtor's prison*), public sentiment again turned toward the honest-money principles long advocated by Thomas Jefferson. Unfortunately, the "Jeffersonian Republicans" (formerly the champions of honest money) had abandoned their post. It took nearly a decade before one man (Andrew Jackson) was able to gain power and defend those principles once again.

Elected President in 1828, Jackson pledged to resurrect honest money, **abolish The 2nd Bank of the United States** and (in so doing) rid our nation of a threat he deemed *"...more formidable and dangerous than a naval and military power of the enemy."* But ridding America of this "formidable and dangerous" threat would be no easy task. Jackson was in for a war.

The Bank had a lot of *friends* in Congress and Biddle regularly rewarded those friends with *assistance* in the business world. Or as Congressman John Randolph put it: *"Every man you meet in this House...with some rare exceptions...is either a stockholder, president, cashier, clerk or doorkeeper, runner, engraver, paper maker, or mechanic in some other way to a bank...The banks are so linked together with the business of the world, that there are very few men exempt from their influence."*

Biddle had fought hard to obtain his position of power. From his scholastic achievements (completing his University of Pennsylvania studies by age 13 and graduating Princeton, valedictorian, at age 15), to his involvement in creating the 2nd Bank of the United States, to the privileges he now enjoyed as its President. He wasn't going to simply put it all down and walk away.

Andrew Jackson had fought hard as well, but his *battles* were more literal. He'd been tortured and starved as a British prisoner during the American War for Independence, he survived the loss of his immediate family (orphaned at 14), he'd been shot in countless gun fights and still carried bullets around in his body. He wasn't going to roll over for anyone, especially a privileged class of "bankers" looking to take control of the country he helped create.

Each man knew the other's aim, the stakes couldn't be higher, and the lines were drawn. (There would be no *peaceful compromise*.) Although the war between these two powerful men *technically* began when Jackson was elected President in 1828, it took a while for things to really heat up.

In 1832, Biddle went in for the kill. The charter for his bank wasn't set to expire until 1836, but in a brilliant political move he persuaded his *friends* in Congress to pass a bill granting his bank an *early* renewal. With Jackson up for reelection, Biddle *assumed* Jackson wouldn't defy Congress and veto the bill. (The controversy could easily cost him a second term as President.)

By Biddle's calculations, this one move put Jackson in checkmate. The Bank would coast into 1836 with another 20-year charter already signed into law and there was little (if anything) Jackson could do about it. Sadly for Biddle, he "calculated" wrong. The law granting early renewal only infuriated Jackson. The President stood his ground.

> "Jackson decided to place his entire political career on the line for this one issue and, with perhaps the most passionate message ever delivered to Congress by any President, before or since, he vetoed the measure.
>
> ...Congress, the banks, speculators, industrialists, and segments of the press; these were the forces commanded by Biddle. But Jackson had a secret weapon which had never been used before in American politics. That weapon was a direct appeal to the voters. He took his message on the campaign trail and delivered it in words well chosen to make a lasting impression...

He spoke out against a moneyed aristocracy which had invaded the halls of Congress, impaired the morals of the people, threatened their liberty, and subverted the electoral process. The Bank, he said, was a hydra-headed monster eating the flesh of the common man. He swore to do battle with the monster and slay it or be slain by it.

...Jackson had awakened the indignation of the American people. When the November ballots were cast, he received a mammoth vote of confidence. He received 55% of the popular vote...and eighty per cent of the vote in the Electoral College. ...Jackson won the election, but the Bank had four more years to operate, and it intended to use those years to sway public sentiment back to its support. The biggest battles were yet to come."

After Jackson won reelection, he wasted no time mounting his attack. He instructed his Treasury Secretary to put all *future* federal deposits in various state-run banks. Moreover, he ordered all federal expenses to be paid (first) out of the remaining funds still held in the 2nd Bank of the United States. With no new deposits coming in, and with the government's existing account drained to zero, the Bank would surely be crushed.

But Jackson's Treasury Secretary (Louis McLane) refused the order. Undeterred, Jackson replaced him with a new Treasury Secretary (William Duane) and instructed him to do the same. But Duane *also* refused the order and, worse, he refused to resign! Not a problem. Duane received the following from the President himself: *"Your further services as Secretary of the Treasury are no longer required."* And with that, the third Treasury Secretary, Roger Taney, took his post. ...And federal funds began moving out of the Bank.

Convinced he finally had "the monster" where he wanted it, Jackson is reported to have said: *"I have it chained...I am ready with the screws to draw every tooth and then the stumps...Mr. Biddle and his Bank* (ought to be) *quiet and harmless as a lamb in six weeks."* But the President's optimism was premature.

Biddle Deliberately Crashes the Economy

"Biddle responded, not like a lamb, but more like a wounded lion. His plan was to rapidly contract the nation's money supply and create another panic-depression similar to the one the Bank had created thirteen years earlier. This then could be blamed on Jackson's withdrawal of federal deposits, and the resulting backlash surely would cause Congress to override the President's veto."

Historian Robert Remini writes:

"Biddle counterattacked. He initiated a general curtailment of loans throughout the entire banking system... It marked the beginning of a bone-crushing struggle between a powerful financier and a determined and equally powerful politician. (Biddle) knew that if he brought enough pressure and agony to the money market, only then could he force the President to restore the deposits. He almost gloated:

> '*This worthy President thinks that because he has scalped Indians and imprisoned Judges, he is to have his way with the Bank. He is mistaken.*
>
> *...**Nothing but widespread suffering** will produce any effect on Congress...Our only safety is in pursuing a steady course of firm restriction – and I have no doubt that such a course will ultimately lead to restoration of the currency and the re-charter of the Bank...*' " (*Emphasis added.*)

What words are there to describe the amazing arrogance and depravity of such men? That they exist at all (and that we have handed them so much power) is enough to make any moral human being shudder in disgust.

With the well-being of millions of citizens in the palm of his hand, Biddle saw no obligation to protect them from harm. Rather, he sadistically tightened his grip. And after crushing enough families to cause "widespread suffering," he (backed by many in the press and Congress) pointed to **Jackson** as the culprit!

In no uncertain terms, Biddle and the Bank were put forward as the *saviors*; the only ones who could possibly *fix* the economy that *Jackson* had broken. And to help ease *the suffering*, they were ready, willing and able to "*assist.*" All they needed was for Congress to overrule Jackson, restore the deposits he'd removed, and re-charter the bank.

> "By the time Congress reconvened in December, in what was called the 'Panic Session,' the nation was in an uproar. Newspapers editorialized with alarm, and letters of angry protest flooded into Washington. ...it

began to look like Biddle's plan would work. In the public eye, it was Jackson who was solely responsible for the nation's woes. It was *his* arrogant removal of Secretary Duane; it was *his* foolish insistence on removing the deposits; it was *his* obstinate opposition to Congress.

For one-hundred days a 'phalanx of orators' daily excoriated the President for his arrogant and harmful conduct. ...a resolution of censure was introduced into the Senate and, on March 28, 1834, it was passed by a vote of 26 to 20. This was the first time that a President had ever been censured by Congress, and it was a savage blow to Jackson's pride.

The President rumbled around the White House in a fit of rage. '*You are a den of vipers,*' he said to a delegation of the Bank's supporters. '*I intend to rout you out and by the Eternal God I will rout you out!*'"

A less determined man would have surrendered, but Jackson only redoubled his efforts. Slowly but surely, public awareness grew that it was *Biddle*, not Jackson, who was to blame for the nation's suffering. Ironically, Biddle's giant ego (and equally big mouth) played a prominent role in exposing the truth.

Biddle was so proud of his *brilliant plan* to crash the economy, he openly bragged about it. And when people heard him brag, and then saw him actually *implement* the plan, they spoke out against what he had done. (Imagine that.) The tables turned once and for all when the Governor of the Bank's home state

(George Wolf of Pennsylvania) publicly denounced both Biddle and the Bank. Within days, public sentiment turned permanently and passionately in support of Jackson.

In the House, Democrats introduced a series of resolutions to show support for the President's policy toward the Bank. A resolution stating the Bank "ought not to be re-chartered" passed with a vote of 134 – 82. That federal deposits in the Bank "ought not to be restored" passed with a vote of 118 – 103. That a special committee of Congress ought to investigate whether the Bank deliberately caused the economic crisis passed with a vote of 175 – 42! Jackson had been vindicated. Even the Senate's vote of censure was eventually rescinded.

As for Biddle:

> "When the investigating committee arrived at the Bank's doors in Philadelphia armed with a subpoena to examine the books, Biddle flatly refused. Nor would he allow inspection of correspondence with Congressmen relating to their personal loans and advances. ...For lesser mortals, such action would have resulted in...stiff fines or imprisonment. But not for Nicholas Biddle. Remini explains:

> "The committeemen demanded a citation for contempt, but many southern Democrats opposed this extreme action, and refused to cooperate. As Biddle bemusedly observed, it would be ironic if he went to prison *'by the votes of members of Congress because I would not give up to their enemies their confidential letters.'*

The ending of this saga holds no surprises. The Bank's charter expired in 1836 and it was restructured as a state bank by the Commonwealth of Pennsylvania. After a spree of speculation in cotton, lavish advances to the Bank's officers, and the suspension of payment in specie, Biddle was arrested and charged with fraud. Although not convicted, he was still undergoing civil litigation when he died."

Where do we stand today?

The Congress has the power to abolish the Federal Reserve System, but our *leaders* have been ominously silent on the issue. It seems few in Washington are interested in cutting off the hand that feeds their insatiable appetite for money and power. Each election the pro-establishment candidates promise us "change" but nothing ever changes and *nothing ever will* until we take from them (and their masters) the power to create limitless piles of money "out of thin air." This money is not only inherently corrupt; it is *the* corrupting force destroying our country.

Today, the Federal government of these "United States" is an abomination. It has more in common with the USSR of yesterday than the founding principles of LIMITED *servant government* enshrined in our Constitution and Bill of Rights. At the highest levels, its members ignore with impunity the "supreme law" they swore an oath to preserve, protect, and defend. Not even the illusion of accountability remains.[22] What Jackson fought so hard to prevent (a federal

---

22 Taken from *Ron Paul and the Future: Nothing has changed.*

government dependent on and controlled by wealthy *special interests*) has come to pass.

The good news is that our ability to spread information and organize is greater today than ever before. If Jackson was able to "wake the people up" and stir them to action (despite powerful interests working against him and no modern technology to help him out), we can too. In fact, all evidence indicates the *awakening* has already begun.

The spirit of Jackson returns (and the people respond)

Prior to 2007, few people knew what the "Federal Reserve System" was, let alone had any idea why they should care. That changed when an honest-money presidential candidate (Ron Paul) came along and showed them the dangers of *dishonest money.* Just as Jackson before him, Ron Paul stood before millions of voters and said something they hadn't heard before: The Central Bank of the United States must be abolished.

Ron Paul's message of freedom and limited government (and the honest money *necessary* to restore and secure them both) drew young and old, black and white, Conservatives, Liberals, Independents, Libertarians, Constitutionalists, and all stripes in between to his cause. Tired of partisan distractions, informed voters joined forces to "strike the root" of our country's problems. They got organized (on their own) and soon a small army stood behind Paul and his message.

Needless to say, the "pro-establishment" elites were less than thrilled with Paul's efforts to undo all of their hard work. For months his campaign was subjected to a nearly total media blackout. However, thanks to the Internet, the "ignore him and nobody will know he exists" tactic didn't work. Paul's message was not only *getting out*, it was *sinking in*. Online polls and other metrics (like how many people were visiting Ron Paul's website and how many people were searching his name) showed support far greater than what the media's coverage implied. The *small army* was growing exponentially.

When they couldn't ignore him, the pro-establishment media began marginalizing Paul and his supporters. They tried to link him to Nazi racists. They ran false stories claiming all of his online support was fraudulent – that it was coming from a handful of Internet "spammers" who were manipulating polls and search statistics. (That lie crumbled when his rallies and campaign coffers began bursting at the seams.) In the debates, his opponents would get 10 minutes of time to speak for every 3 minutes of time he was given. Moderators, along with some of his opponents, openly mocked him and laughed out loud as he spoke. It was disgraceful, but telling. Only a fool would have doubted that there was a concerted effort to shut him down.

Despite ALL of this, Ron Paul raised over **33 MILLION** dollars for his campaign. More impressive, nearly every penny came from individual donors like you and me, instead of from the usual *special interests* looking to buy influence. By the end, he secured more than 1 million votes and even beat "media darlings" like Rudy Giuliani and John McCain in multiple contests. But that's still not the most amazing part of this story...

What's most amazing is how quickly the people responded to Ron Paul's unique and (by normal "sound bite" political standards) complex message. He announced his candidacy in March of 2007. In less than a year he'd raised well over 30 millions dollars and had supporters all over America (*and all around the world*).

In short, "The Establishment," with all their power and influence, *barely* slowed a grass-roots effort that had only 1 year to organize and grow. What can they possibly do against a 2, 3, 4, or 5-year effort? What can they do when, instead of just a few million citizens, 30 or 40 million know the truth about *the system* they've been using against us? NOTHING, that's what. They, like those before them, will be defeated.

And here is where you come into the picture.

This Campaign for Liberty[23] is bigger than Ron Paul, it's bigger than you and me; it's even bigger than the United States. Using their dishonest money, an **unelected** "*intellectual elite and world bankers*" are perverting governments around the world to serve their own ends. They're "arrogant, brilliant, and ruthless" and they'll stop at nothing to finish what they have started. That is why **WE** must stop them. And by exposing (and destroying) their greatest weapon, we will.

Visit DishonestMoney.com for more information on The Federal Reserve System, including free videos and audio, links to related groups & websites or to obtain a discount on "multiple-copy" purchases of Dishonest Money: Financing the Road to Ruin.

---

23 See Ron Paul's website: CampaignForLiberty.com

• "...they who control the credit of the nation direct the policy of Governments and hold in the hollow of their hands the destiny of the people." **–Reginald McKenna, Midlands Bank of England**

• "The real truth of the matter is, as you and I know, that a financial element in the larger centers has owned the Government ever since the days of Andrew Jackson...The country is going through a repetition of Jackson's fight with the Bank of the United States — only on a far bigger and broader basis. **–President Franklin D. Roosevelt** in a letter to Edward M. House

• "Since I entered politics, I have chiefly had men's views confided to me privately. Some of the biggest men in the United States...are afraid of somebody, are afraid of something. They know that there is a power somewhere so organized, so subtle, so watchful, so interlocked, so complete, so pervasive, that they had better not speak above their breath when they speak in condemnation of it. **–President Woodrow Wilson** in his book, *The New Freedom*

• "By a continuing process of inflation, governments can confiscate, secretly and unobserved, an important part of the wealth of their citizens... There is no subtler, no surer means of overturning the existing basis of society than to debauch the currency. The process engages all the hidden forces of economic law on the side of destruction, and does it in a manner which not one man in a million is able to diagnose."**–John Maynard Keynes** in his book, The Economic Consequences of the Peace

• "The bankers own the earth. Take it away from them, but leave them the power to create money, and with the flick of the pen they will create enough deposits to buy it back again. However, take it away from them, and all the great fortunes like mine will disappear and they ought to disappear, for this would be a happier and better world to live in. But, if you wish to remain the slaves of bankers and pay the cost of your own slavery, let them continue to create money."–**Attributed to Josiah Charles Stamp, former Director of the Bank of England** (Some question whether Stamp ever actually said this. If he didn't, it's a shame. This happens to be one of the most accurate and concise statements ever written on modern banking.)

ADDENDUM

Ten Humans and a Banker

Ten humans decide they want to start their own community, but they have no common "money" to build their economy on. A banker from a nearby town agrees to *help them out*. He loans each person $10 (money that he simply "prints up" in his basement) and agrees to accept "interest only" payments on the loans at a rate of 10%. (A tiny $1.00 interest payment per person, per year.)

So, the new community begins with a *total* money supply of $100. Prices in the community are set according to this money supply and everything seems fine.

At the end of the first year, the banker gathers everyone together to collect his interest. Each of the ten people surrenders their $1 "interest only" payment, but none of them stops to consider that, after making the payment, all ten of them *still owe* the banker $10 each. How can everyone pay their debt if the community's total money supply is now only $90? There are no longer enough dollars in circulation to pay the banker the $100 he is owed.

> **Side Note:** The banker *could* spend the $10 worth of interest payments back into the economy and this

would raise the community's money supply back to $100, but he won't do that. For now, the people will be left with only $90 to pay $100 in debt.

Although the common people might not have figured out their debt predicament, *they have* noticed that getting a "fair price" for their products and services seems a little tougher than the year before. Prices seem to be dropping. But the banker understands why. He knows that there are fewer dollars in circulation and this raises the value or "purchasing power" of each dollar. As the value of each dollar goes up, the number of dollars a customer is willing to pay (in exchange for another person's products or services) goes down.

By the end of the second year, one of the borrowers (a successful businessman who has managed to accumulate $15) makes his interest payment *AND* pays off his debt in full. So, as everyone else makes their second $1.00 "interest only" payment, he pays both the interest due and the $10 he originally borrowed. This reduces the community's total money supply by another $20. ($10 in "interest payments" plus the businessman's $10 principal payment.) There are now only 70 dollars (to be shared by all ten people in the community) and nine people still owe the banker the full $10 ($90 in total debt).

Two more years pass and two more people manage to earn enough to pay off their debts. So, by the end of the fourth year, the money supply is reduced by another $38. ($18 in "interest" payments plus another $20 from the two individuals who, despite the difficulty, earned enough from the shrinking money supply to pay off their loans.) There is now only **$32** left in the community, to be shared among all ten people – and seven of those people still owe the banker $10 each ($70 total).

At this point, it will be nearly impossible for those who are still in debt to make their $1.00 interest payments, let alone pay off their debt. (Where once there was $10 for each person in the community, there is now only $3.20.) With so few dollars left in circulation, the purchasing power of each dollar has gone through the roof. Prices have fallen drastically and the economy is in shambles. If the banker does not "help the people out" (by putting more money back into the community), bankruptcies are inevitable; bank seizure of property is inevitable, financial ruin is inevitable. [24]

The businessman (who paid his debt off first) approaches the banker. He explains to the banker that the people *want* to work; it's just that times are tough. At its height, his business employed half the town. Now, he is down to just a couple employees and he has had to cut their pay…he just can't afford the $2.00 per year salary anymore (and even at that rate, HALF of their pay is being eaten up by their annual interest payment. They can barely feed themselves!)

He points out, if the banker agrees to fund a new / ambitious project, the town will spring to life. There will be jobs for all and the suffering will end. But he also points out, without the

---

24 Again, the banker could technically spend ALL of the interest he has collected back into the economy to ease the pressure (quite a deal for him since the dollars he has "*earned*" will now be worth a small fortune), but this does not change the fact that the debt is inescapable. As the debts are paid, the money supply shrinks. Without new loans (new debt) the economy will grind to a halt and those still holding debt will have no choice but default.

project, many people are likely to default on their loans... the businessman just doesn't see how the people will be able to continue making their payments in such a depressed economy. "Please Mr. Banker," he says, "you've got to help us out."

The banker agrees to the loan, and it's a whopper ($100). The businessman is ecstatic. Shaking the banker's hand, he promises to *make good* on the loan. He's not only certain his new venture will be profitable, he's certain the whole town will benefit. "Oh, thank you Mr. Banker" he says sincerely, "you have done a good thing here!"

But nobody stops to think that there is now $132.00 in the economy to cover $170.00 of debt. And each year, $10 in interest will be due on the new $100 loan and $7 will be due on the $70 that was unpaid from before. The banker knows the math...and with a smile he creates the $100 "out of thin air" and the cycle starts over.

Welcome to the "debt-based" monetary system. Whether it is a small community or a powerful nation, any economy built on this fraudulent system is doomed. Its debt is mathematically inescapable and, if the people start paying down their debts (or if the banks simply refuse to renew loans) the money supply will evaporate and financial ruin will follow.

When the Federal Government talks about "paying off the national debt" it is LYING to you. It cannot do this without destroying our economy. The bankers that created our Federal Reserve System in 1913 built "dependency" into the system. It was designed to create ever-expanding, inescapable debt. By inflating (and deflating) the money supply, our wealth (as a nation and as individuals) is at the mercy of the bankers.

We must free ourselves from this monetary system. We must demand honest money.

Government Without Income Tax

Over the years, I've gotten into many discussions with people regarding the intended nature of our Federal Government and how one of the major limitations on its power (the "power of the purse") was subverted in 1913. Specifically, when the "Federal Reserve System" and the "Federal income tax" were created in 1913, they destroyed all reasonable limitations on how much money the Federal Government had access to. Subsequently, they also destroyed all reasonable limitations on the Federal Government's ability to expand far beyond its constitutional role.

When discussing the issue of taxation, the average American has a tendency to defend "income tax" as being necessary to fund government at the Federal level. (Below, that very point is made by a visitor to StopTheLie.com.) Hopefully this short article will put the issue into its proper perspective.

Assertion:

As for the income tax, only an anarchist thinks a country can survive without taxation.

My Rebuttal:

These are two separate issues. One, the issue of needing "taxes" to finance government. Two, the issue of whether or not an INCOME tax is needed to finance our FEDERAL Government.

Few Americans realize that this country DID NOT have a Federal *income tax* prior to 1913. Think about that for a minute. America went from being a "start up" (in 1776) to the most prosperous nation on the planet without an "income tax." (Let alone the intrusive, bloated and, dare I say, "unconstitutional" government that goes with it.)

Corporate taxes, taxes on alcohol, tobacco, firearms, tariffs on trade, military hardware sales, etc.; these would be more than enough to fund the "constitutionally limited" Federal Government established by our founding fathers. Or, to put it another way, if the income tax was abolished today, the Federal government would still have over a TRILLION dollars annually to fund its operations. (Even after *adjusting for inflation*, this is still an obscene amount of money compared to what it used to operate on.)

Also, few realize that a huge percentage of the income taxes collected do nothing to fund government programs. The money is simply burned away as interest payments on the debt that our "leaders" have accumulated for us. Whatever benefit (real or imagined) the borrowed money was supposed to have, the actual cost of all those programs increases drastically when you include the added expense of interest payments. How much is added? Currently, interest payments on our 10 TRILLION dollar debt are costing

American taxpayers about 50 million dollars PER HOUR. That is every hour of every day, every week of every year. (Approximately $450 Billion a year.)

Now, you'd think our elected officials would be a little worried about this. You'd think they'd want to get rid of the national debt and "free up" all that money currently being wasted on interest payments. Instead, they continue to spend money like there is no tomorrow. More specifically, they are currently adding more than 60 million dollars PER HOUR to the debt we already have.

Do the majority of Americans consider this acceptable? Very unlikely, but it doesn't matter because we can no longer "turn off" the spigot. Those who engineered the system we've been living under, since 1913, were careful to make sure of that.

You see, the "income tax" is just part of the equation. The other part (also created in 1913) is the Federal Reserve Banking System. This central bank was created to act as an exclusive lender to our ambitious friends in Washington DC. Now, instead of having to go to the American people for money, the government could just go to their friends at the Federal Reserve. And "The Fed" bankers would be happy to *loan* whatever was requested.

To put the importance of this arrangement into perspective, consider the following:

When you and I "give money" to the government, it COSTS us money. You and I have to actually earn wages before we can hand them over and, in handing them over, our financial power is depleted. When the bankers give money to the government, they EARN money. Unlike us, bankers can simply print whatever the government needs prior to handing it over and, in handing it over, their financial power (in the form of interest payments) is enhanced.

So, the bigger the government gets and the more debt it acquires, the greater the burden on you and me. On the other side of the equation, the bigger the government gets and the more debt it acquires, the greater the benefit to the bankers. Where government spending and debt costs us our wealth, government spending and debt makes them theirs. It goes without saying that this system is antithetical to the concept of "limited government."

The Creature from Jekyll Island, written by G. Edward Griffin, is perhaps the single best resource I've seen regarding this dangerous partnership. It not only covers how the takeover of 1913 was engineered but it also covers the goals of the international bankers who made it all happen. Their final aim is nothing less than the destruction of American sovereignty and merger of all nations into a financially controlled "one world government." To read this book is to learn more (in 20 hours or so) than a lifetime of "public schooling" or "mainstream news" would ever teach you. It is everything the criminal elite don't want you to know about their anti-American agenda.

Now, back to where this all started: Can we support our Federal Government without an income tax? That depends. The corrupt, overgrown, unconstitutional government we currently have? Absolutely not. The constitutionally limited government America was supposed to have? Absolutely.

And if we don't gain control of this "creature" that is feeding on our country, we will inadvertently facilitate the destruction of everything America was meant to be. Rest assured that won't happen by accident; it will come to us *by design*.

We Have the Advantage

Taking a serious look at government wrong-doing is no easy task. Not because the damning evidence is hard to find, but because the truth (once found) is very hard to swallow. How does one reconcile the fact that we are being led into slavery (and to slaughter) by a group of pathological liars who, ironically, have been appointed to "protect us?"

How does one come to grips with the fact there are still millions of Americans who believe there is a *good* half of the government and a *bad* half? An intellectual twilight zone where *good* has nothing to do with the ACTIONS of elected officials and everything to do with whether or not they've dressed themselves in blue or red.

As I began my journey into the bottomless pit of government tyranny and lies I was shocked to find things were much worse than I had originally imagined. Even more upsetting, I came to understand that my 30 years of ignorant bliss had been carefully manufactured on an assembly line of distractions and disinformation. My ignorance had been no accident; it had been *the goal* of the system.

After a few years of serious digging, I reached a point where I couldn't help but stand in awe at the amount of dirt I'd unearthed. I thought to myself, *"How the Hell can all of this be going on and so few know about it?"* The logical answer came shortly thereafter: *"It is only going on BECAUSE so few know about it."*

What I had initially hoped was just a rare instance of wrong-doing, turned out to be standard operating procedure. What I hoped was just a new phenomenon (brought about under an exceedingly corrupt administration) turned out to be as old as history itself.

There before me stood the ugly truth: *Government* is "the power to impose your will," *politician* is a synonym for conman, and at the top it's criminals who run the show. The "political system," it turns out, is nothing more than a way for the criminal elite to hide and legitimize their illegitimate behavior. Is it any wonder the worst among us rise to the heights of power? Is it any wonder the most talented liars seize the greatest rewards?

"But wait," you say. *"The title of this piece is: We have the advantage. After seeing the enormity of the problems we face, how can you honestly believe we've got the upper hand?"* Well, it's pretty simple. For a clue, let me borrow from Adolph Hitler's propaganda minister:

> "The lie can be maintained only for such time as the State can shield the people from the political, economic and/or military consequences of the lie. It thus becomes vitally important for the State to use all of its powers to repress dissent, for the truth is the mortal enemy of the lie, and thus by extension, the truth becomes the greatest enemy of the State." – Dr. Joseph M. Goebbels

In short, the State has grown so greedy, so corrupt, so dangerous and belligerent, that it no longer has the power to "shield the people" from the consequences of its lies. Additionally, it has all but lost its ability to bury the mounting evidence against it.

Where before the State could easily silence the masses with clever manipulations like "You're giving aid and comfort to the enemy," now brave citizens are standing up and stating the obvious: *"No, we're giving aid and comfort to the truth."*

We must never forget that liars and thieves depend on ignorance to exist among us. They lose their ability to manipulate and profit at our expense when their tricks and true aims are exposed. So long as we are gaining and spreading awareness, they (by default) are losing power.

If you think about it, the amount of time it took to build the current system of manipulation and control is truly pathetic compared to how quickly it is unraveling. More and more people are waking up every day. They're leaving the mainstream media in droves; they're actually THINKING beyond the false "left / right" paradigm, they're seeking (and finding) the truth of their own volition.

At this point, we are so awash in documented wrong-doing that nearly anyone (in just one month's time) can be shown enough to completely neutralize decades of government brainwashing. The government, on the other hand, enjoys no such luxury. What has taken them decades to create cannot be regained in a month, a year, or even a lifetime. Once a person "sees" the truth with their own eyes, the gig is up.

As a result of this fact, maintaining their hold on power is mathematically impossible.

Our enemy faces an unstoppable and continuous erosion of their power. Information (specifically, the truth) is the weapon that will destroy them. They will tell us otherwise, they will pretend everything is fine and their power is secure, but like everything else they say we will know it isn't true. In the end, their time will come and they will fail. But that should come as no surprise. ...Armed with the truth, we have the advantage. Believe it.

Empower Yourself

> "Think about the implications of your money not buying anything of value. How would you live? You are urban. You are dependent on a complex system of computerized production and distribution. It is all governed by profit and loss." –Gary North

As stated in the quote above, everything in our system is "governed by profit and loss." When an existing system for measuring profit and loss breaks down (when a currency *goes bad*), it takes time for another system to emerge and replace it. During the transition period, products and services that we *take for granted* can become temporarily unavailable.

Obviously, those who have certain "items of value" in their homes will be in far better shape during a monetary collapse than those who don't. For this reason, I'm not going to belabor the point. Nor will I get into detailing the risk of *not* protecting you and your family against other problems that can destabilize the "complex system" that we all depend on... problems like mass unemployment, war, weather, terrorism, pandemics, civil unrest, etc. Instead, I will put forward a simple idea: If too much *dependence* on our system is a problem, a greater degree of *independence* is our solution.

With that in mind, the *least* we should have in our possession is: Storable food, water filters, gold and / or silver bullion and something for self-defense.

Food and water: If you don't have access to food and water, you're in big trouble. You will have no choice but go where you're told to go and eat / drink what you're given. (For a visual of how that might turn out, think: "Hurricane Katrina / Superdome.") If this sounds like something you'd rather avoid, then buy some storable foods. Many storable foods have a shelf life of 15 to 30 years and, believe it or not, they actually taste good. Just add clean water and you will eat well. (Regarding "clean water," you'll want to have a good water filtration system.)

Any amount of storable food is better than nothing. If you can only afford a 2-week supply, then start there. But make it a goal to get at least a 3-month supply stored away as soon as you can. And if you can work your way up to a 6-month or 1-year supply, go for it. (Try to get your close friends and relatives to do the same.)

- I have purchased most of my storable food (and other preparedness items) from **Nitro-pak.com**. This company has agreed to extend a 10% discount to all of my readers. (Just mention the coupon code "dishonestmoney" and you could easily save hundreds of dollars off their already excellent prices.)

- I personally use a Berkey water filtration system. It will purify water from lakes, streams, wells and even stagnant ponds. Additionally, if you have "city water" that is fluoridated, Berkey offers "PF-2" filters that will remove the fluoride. (Not sure why you'd want to remove fluoride from your water? Visit AvoidFluoride.com for a quick overview.) The following Berkey dealer offers excellent prices: **Directive21.com**

Gold and silver bullion: I am not aware of any case in history where a paper currency collapsed and gold / silver was NOT accepted in its place. If there are products and services for sale, gold and silver are virtually guaranteed to buy them. Just like your storable food, you should only "break out the gold / silver coins" when they're necessary. Think of your coins as "storable money" that will increase in value as the collapsing currency loses its value. I recommend that you stick with bullion coins for your "storable-money" fund. [25]

- Midas Resources offers competitive prices on gold and silver coins. The company is "A" rated with the Better Business Bureau and actively educates people about corruption in government. When you're ready to purchase some "real money" (gold and silver), I recommend giving Midas a chance to earn your business. You can reach them at 1-800-686-2237 or you can visit them online at **MidasResources.com**

---

[25]   The value of bullion coins is based solely on their gold or silver content, not on other variables like age, rarity, or condition.

Self-defense: It doesn't make any sense to gather items for you and your family only so, when those items are needed the most, somebody can come along and take them from you. The most effective "self-defense" tool you can own is a gun. If you are afraid of guns, or if you are simply unfamiliar with them, I highly recommend you sign up for a basic firearms training course. Any fear you have now will decrease by about 90% once you gain a few hours of "hands on" experience. If you want to start with something very simple, begin with a revolver.

Of course, you do have other choices for self-defense. A stun gun, stun baton, taser, pepper spray (or bear spray if you want major "pepper power") will greatly improve your ability to defend yourself. They all lack the reach of a firearm, but they are definitely *much better* than nothing and will help in many situations.

These four essentials (food and water, real money, and a way to defend yourself) will help you through nearly any instability that temporarily disrupts the "complex system" we all depend on. Your choice *to be* prepared will not only benefit you and your family, it will also benefit those who chose *not to be*... (You, and millions of others like you, will not take up space in government-run "Superdomes," nor will you need to be fed, watered, and "protected.") In short: The better prepared you are, the better it will be for the nation as a whole.

**Spread the Word about the
"Federal Reserve System"** *Scam*
Bulk Discounts on *Dishonest Money* are available
at:
DishonestMoney.com

Made in the USA
Lexington, KY
15 June 2011